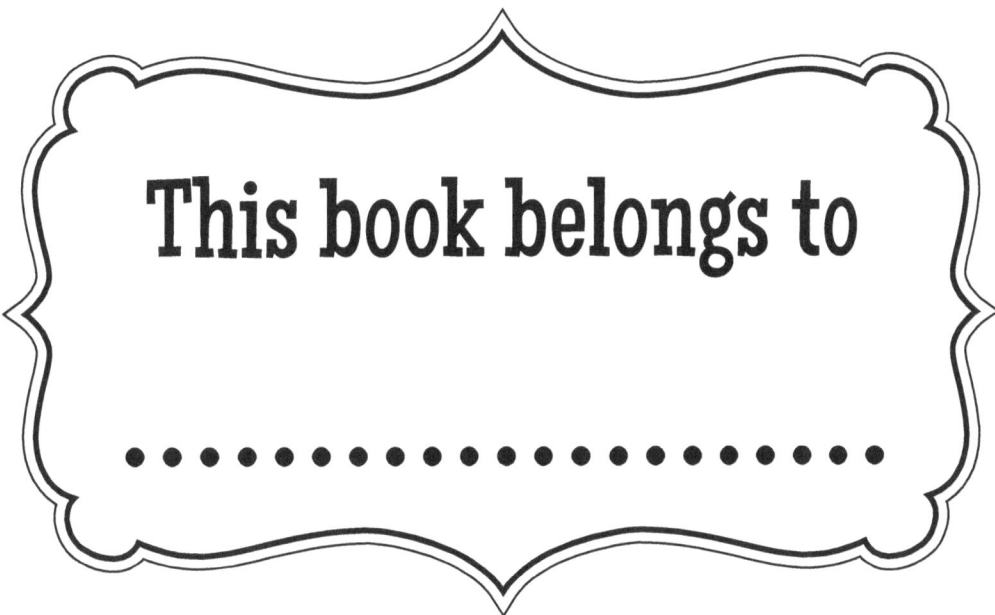

This book belongs to
....

Copyright © 2020 by Lekicia Knight

All rights reserved. No part of this publication may be reproduced or distributed in any form or any means without the written permission of the owner.

ISBN: 9798578451140

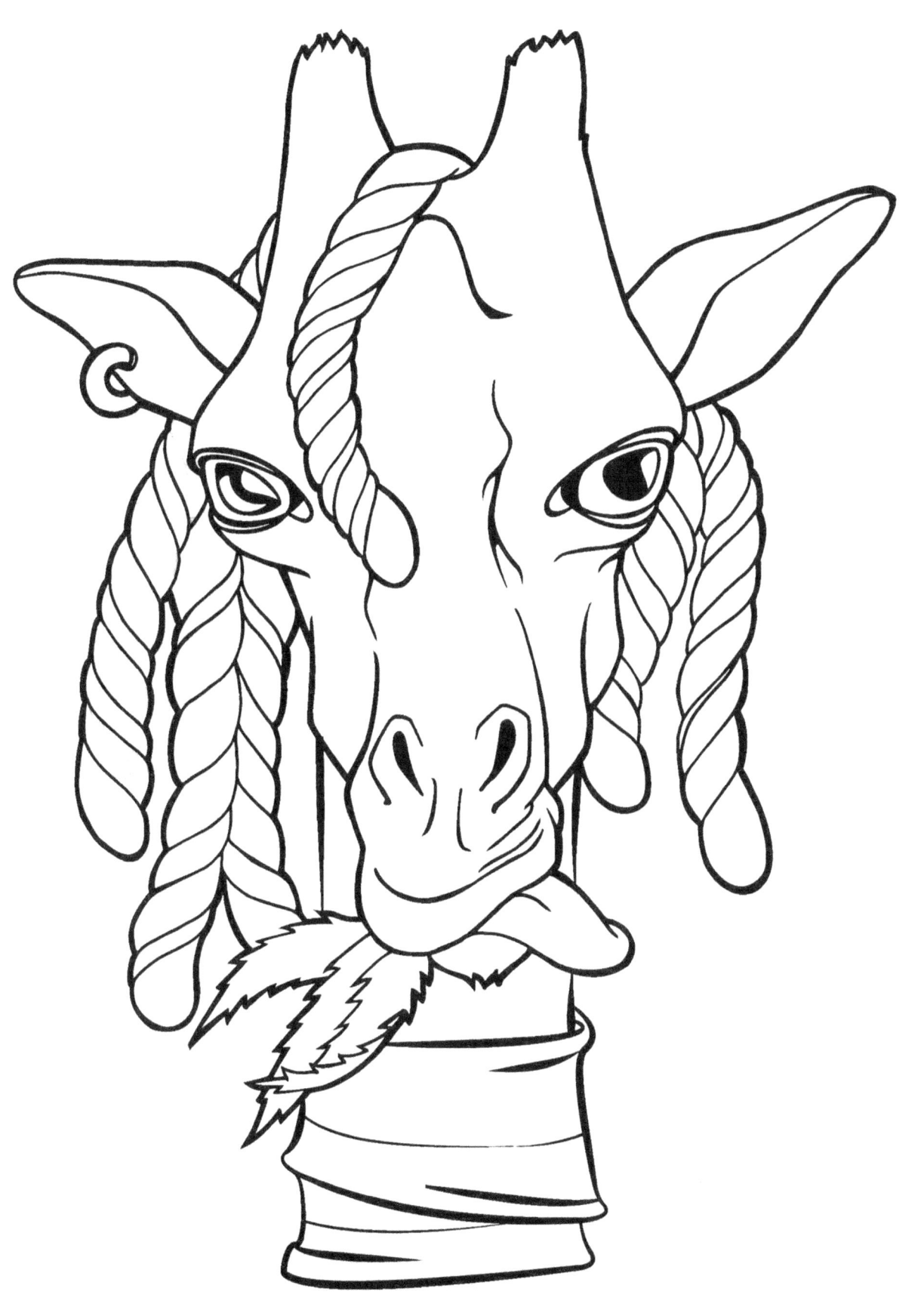

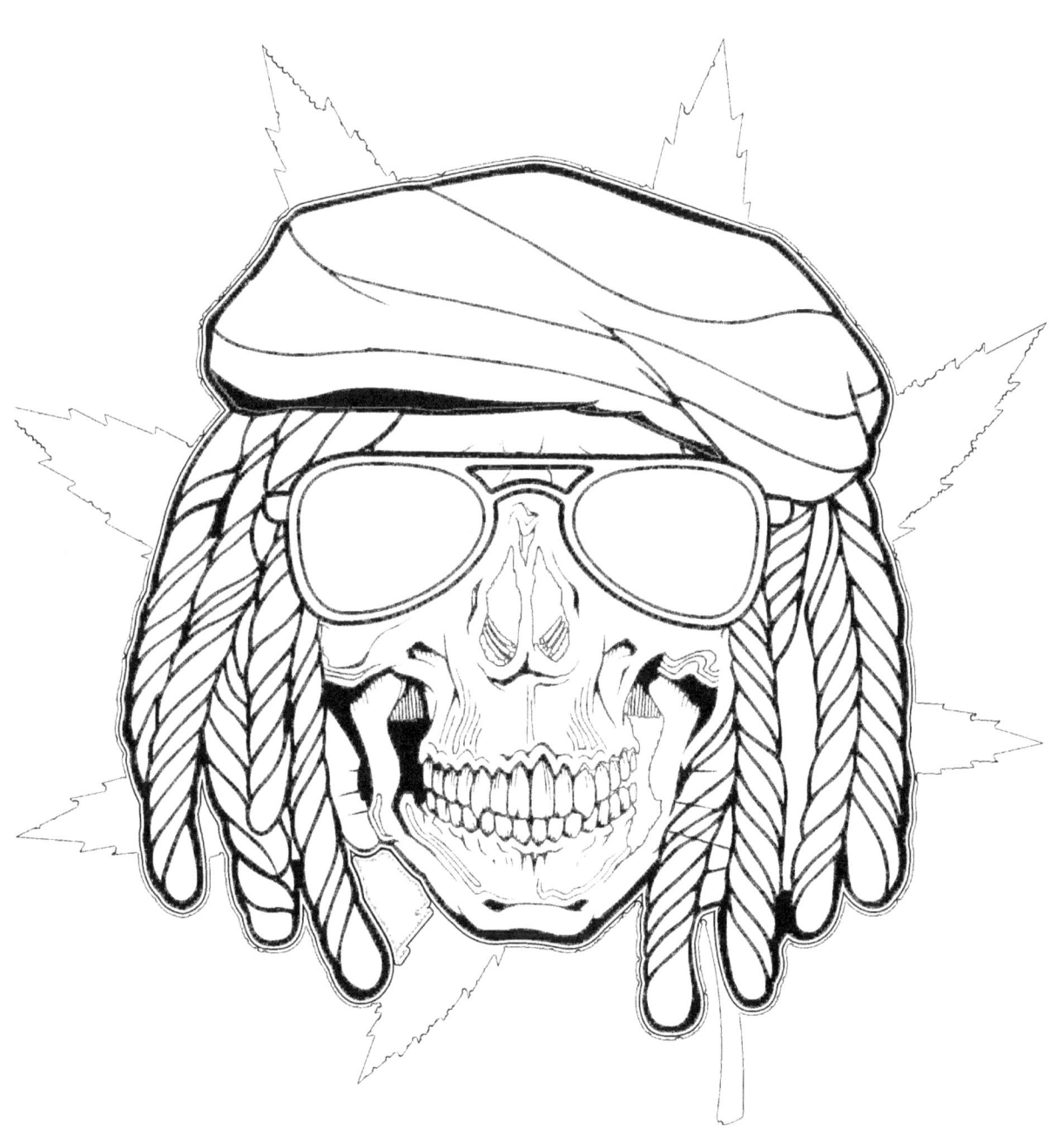

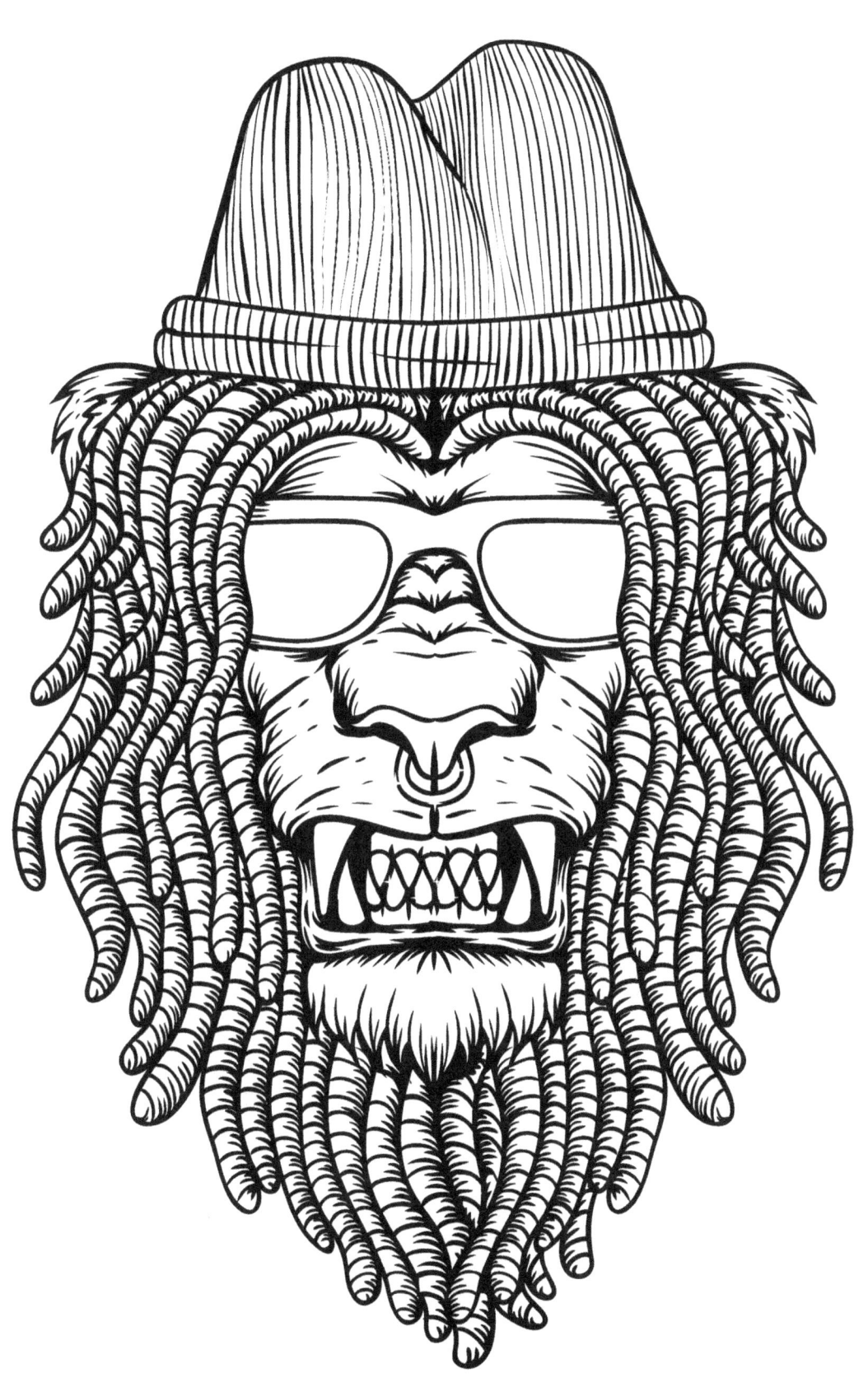

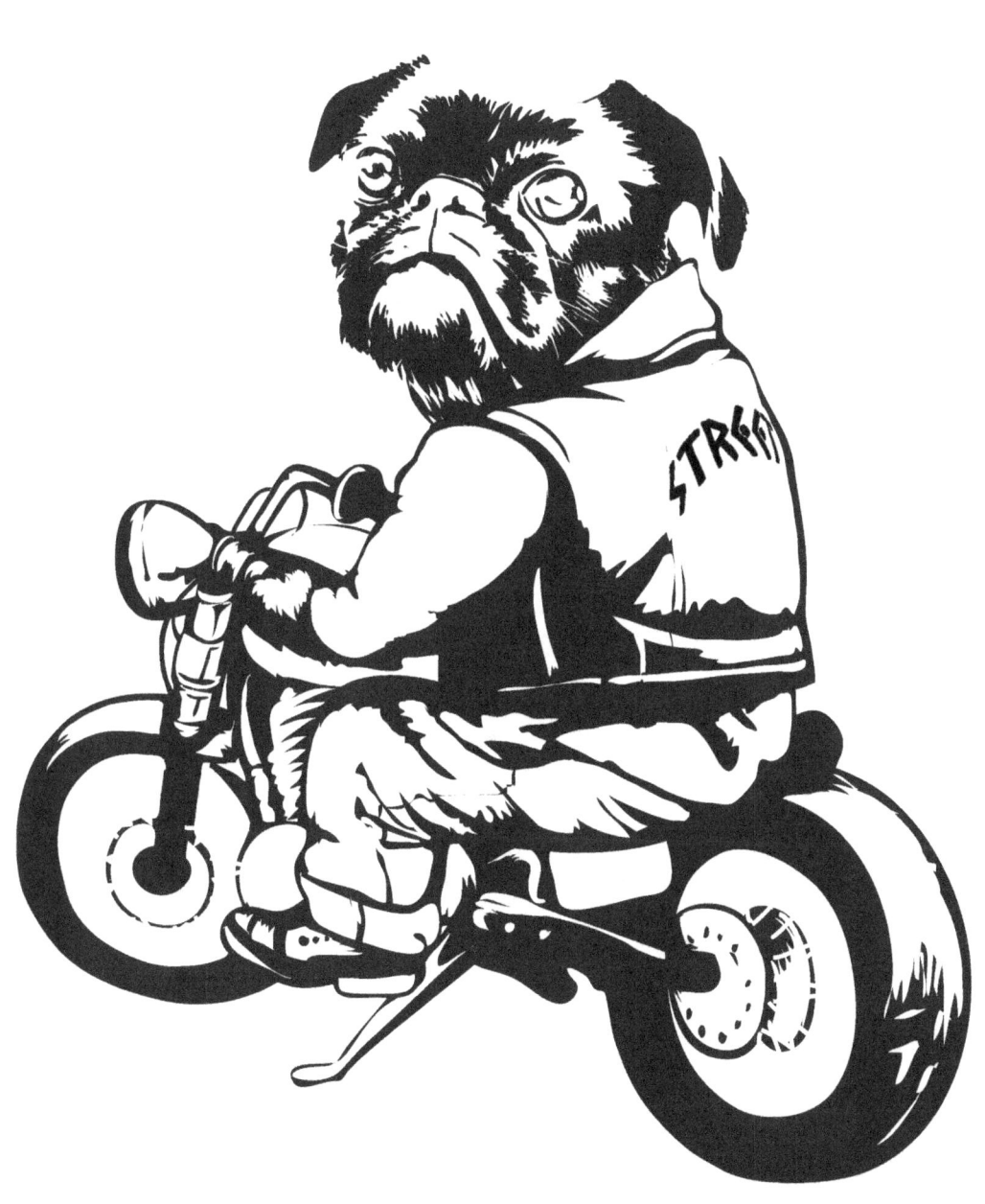

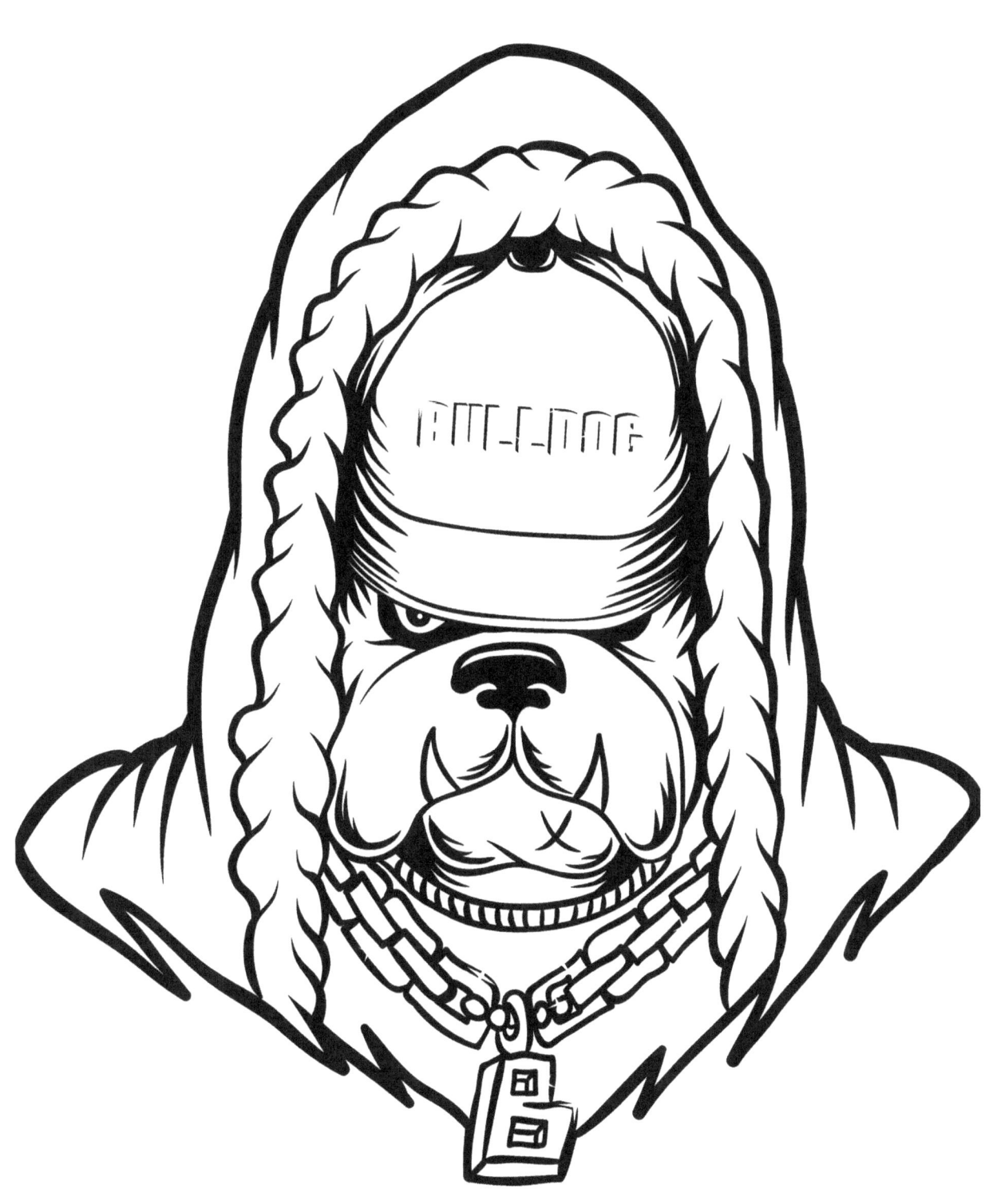

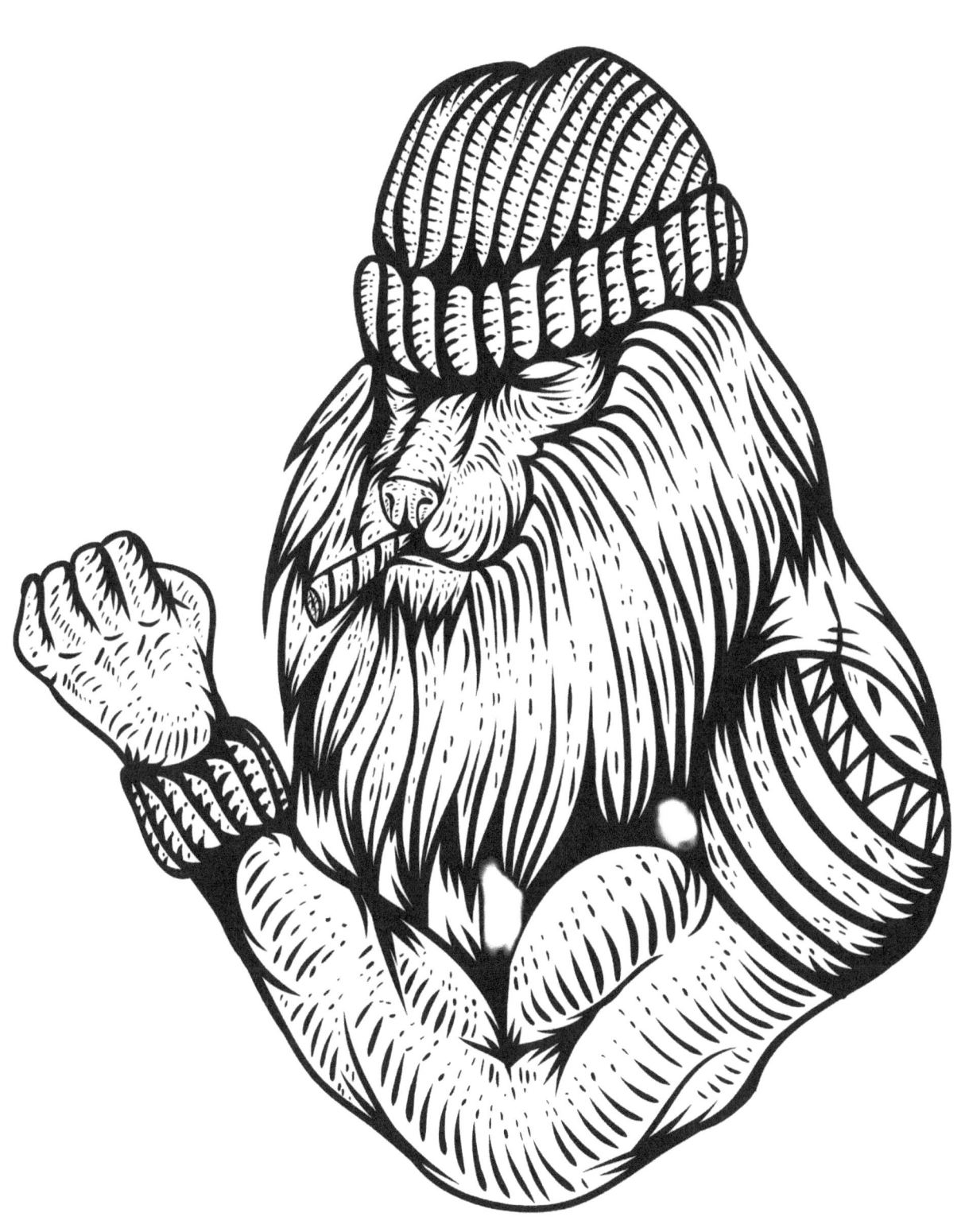

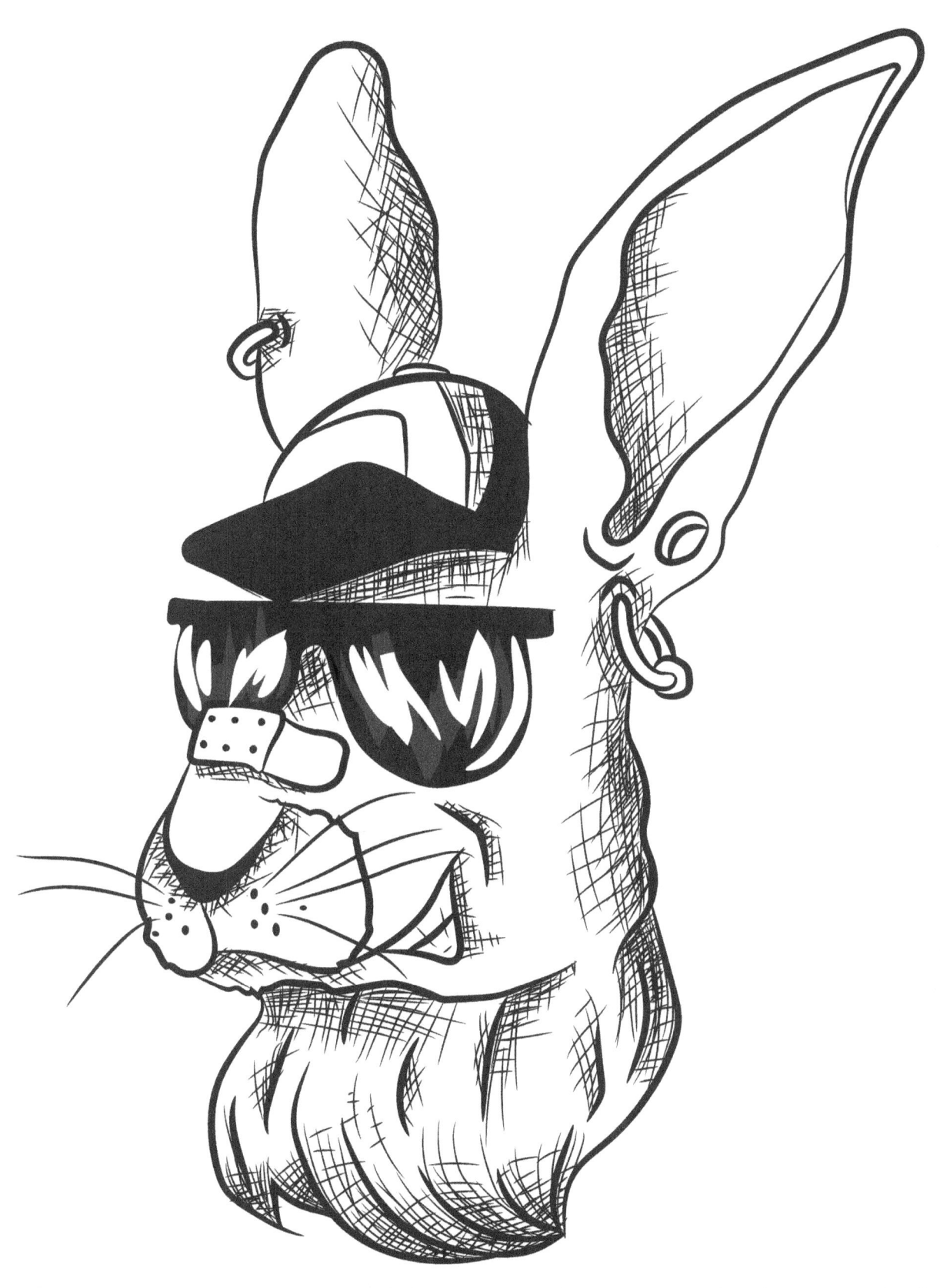

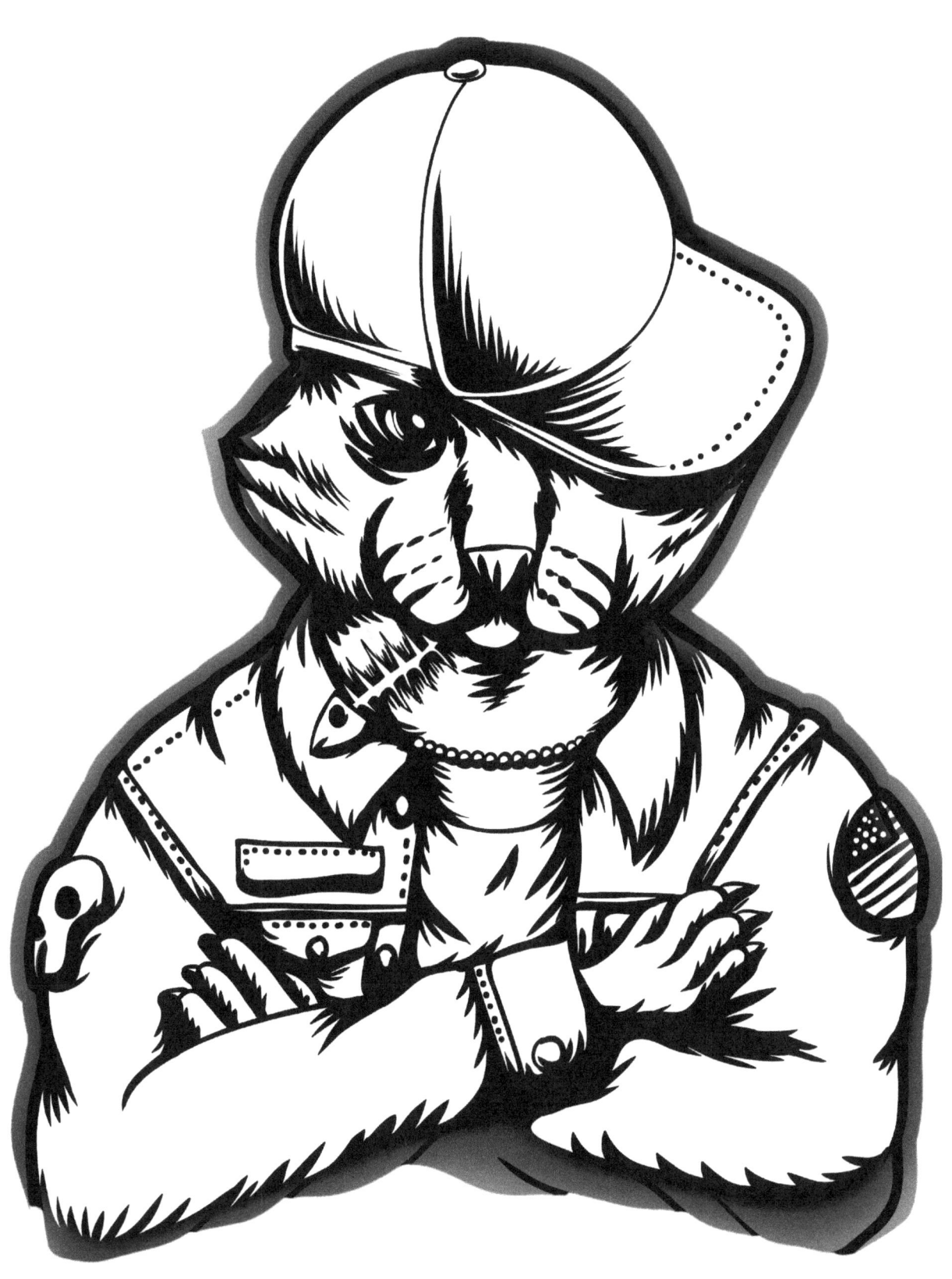

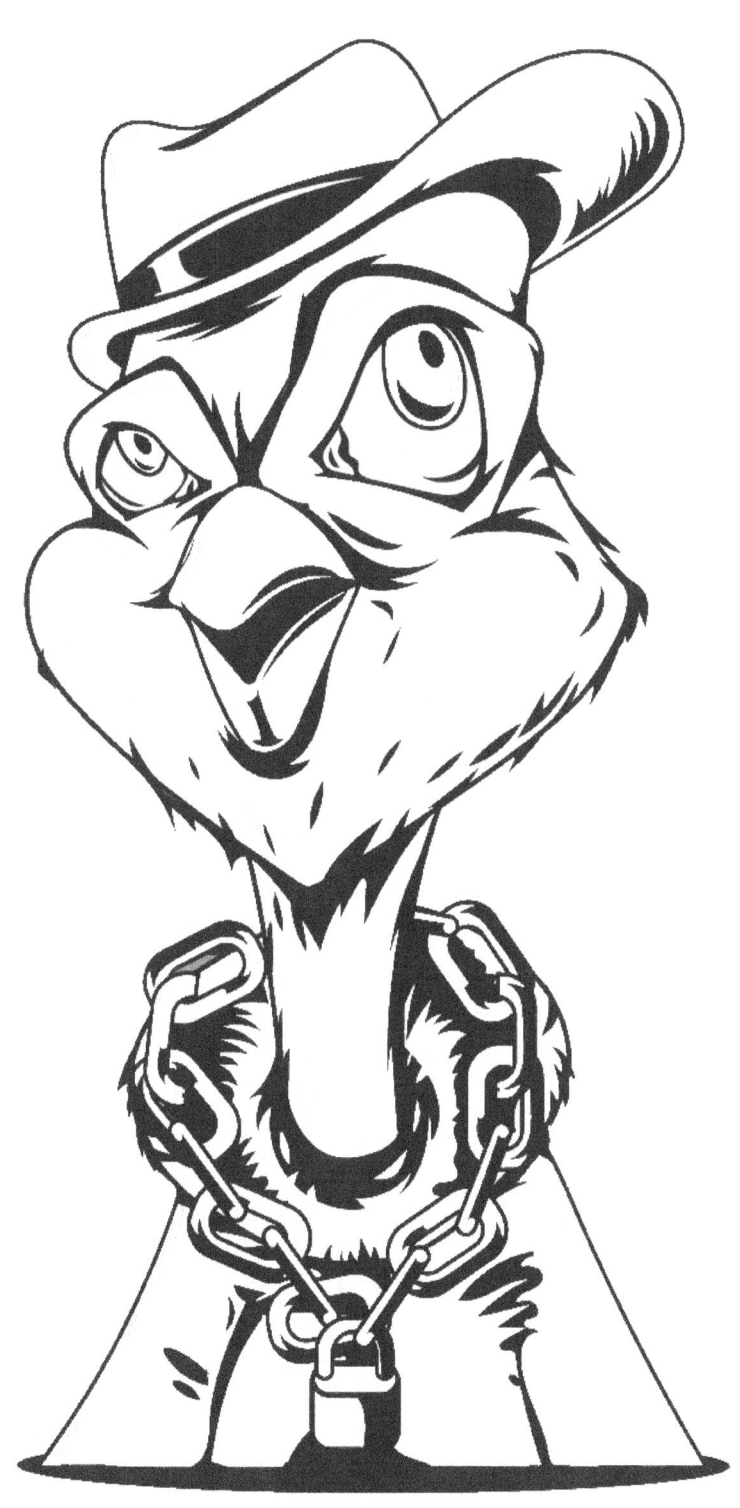

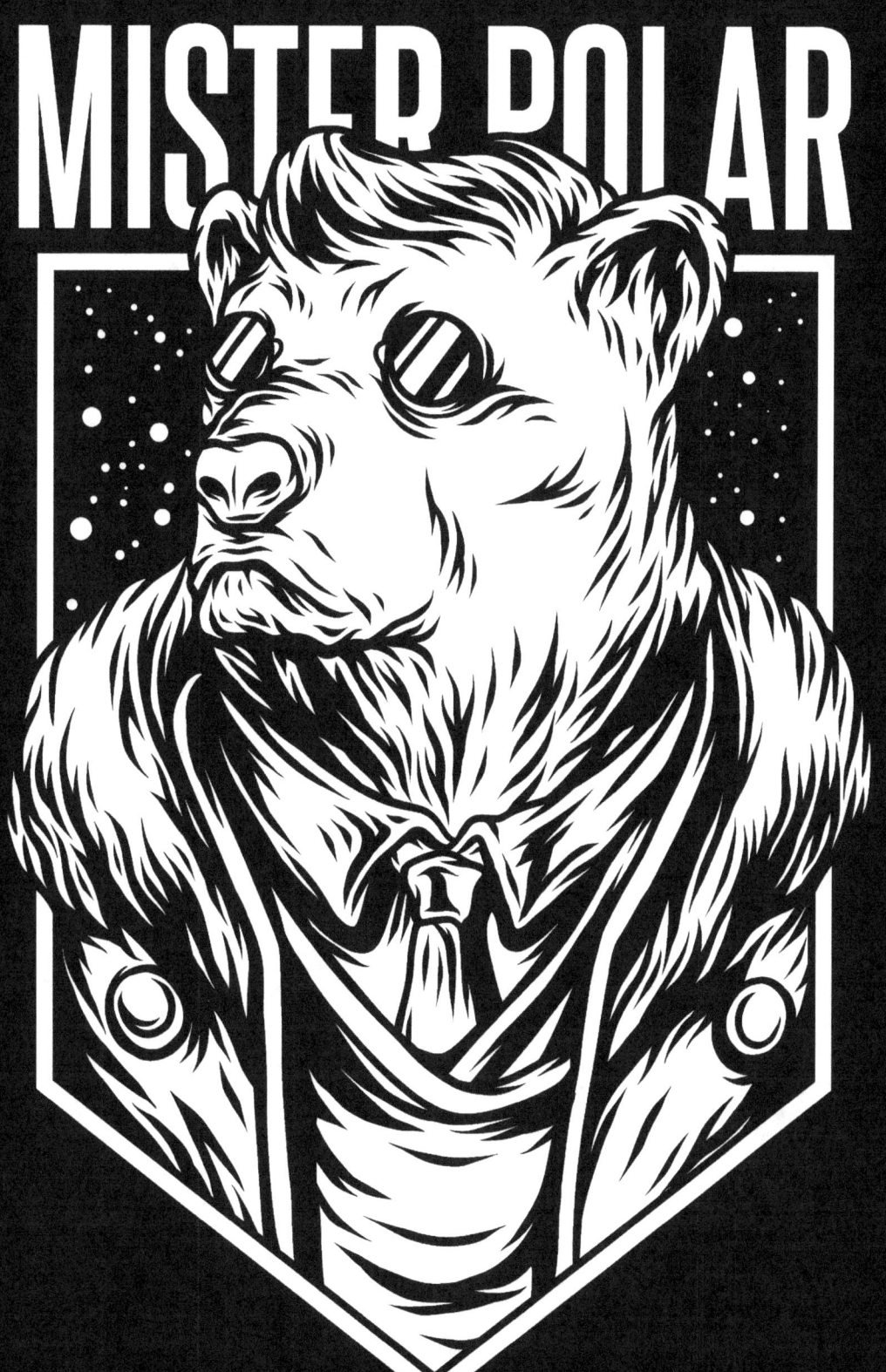

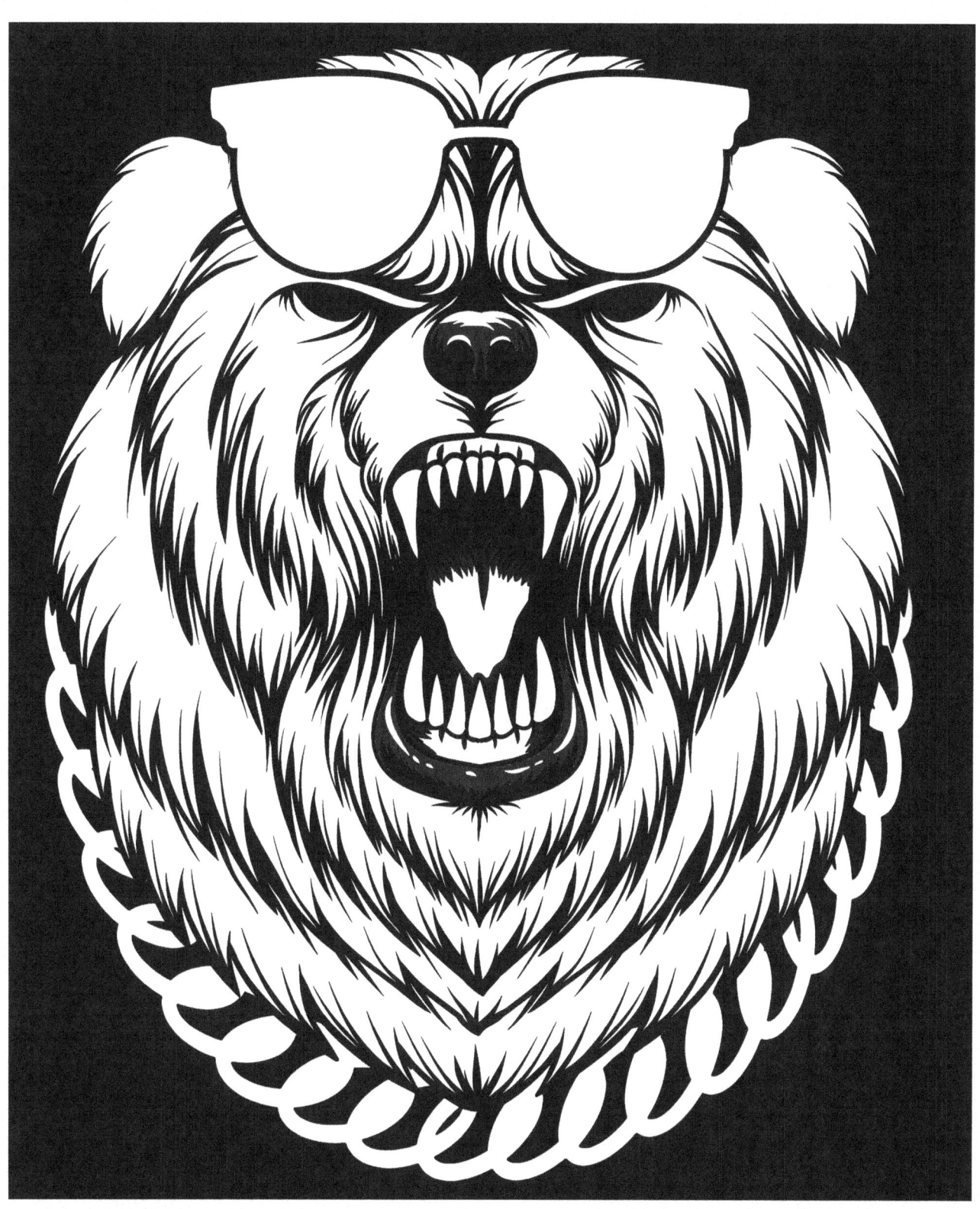

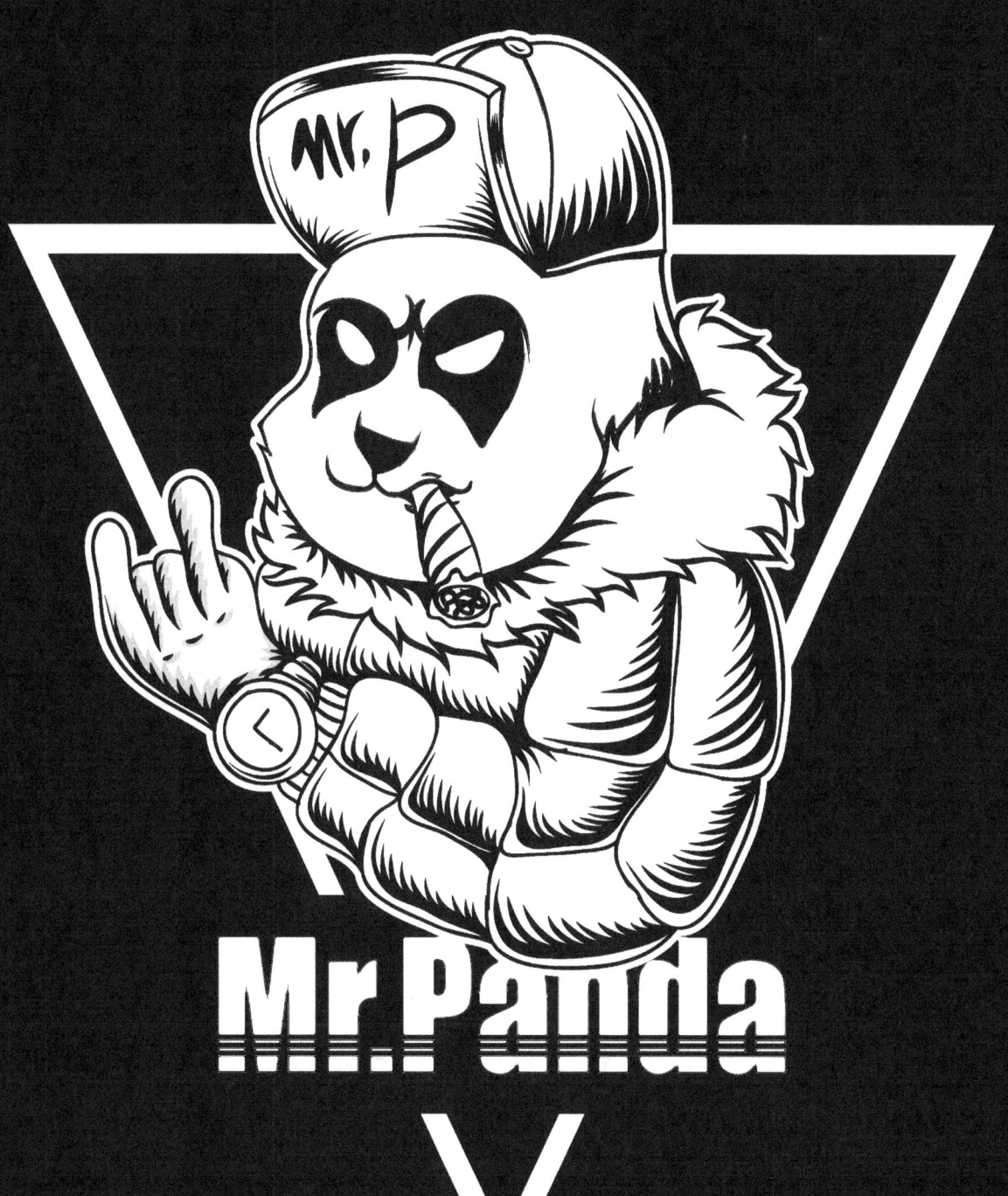

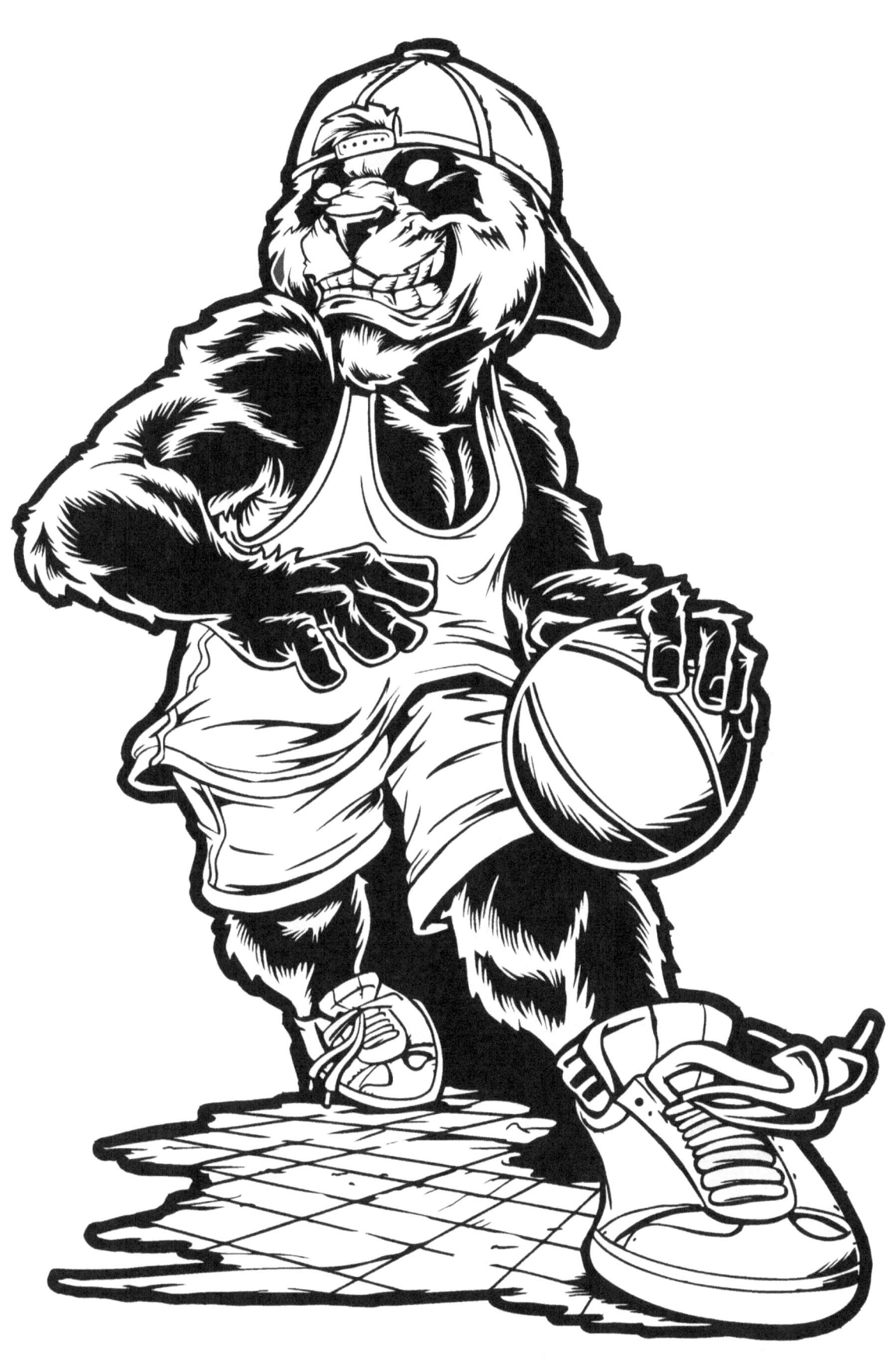

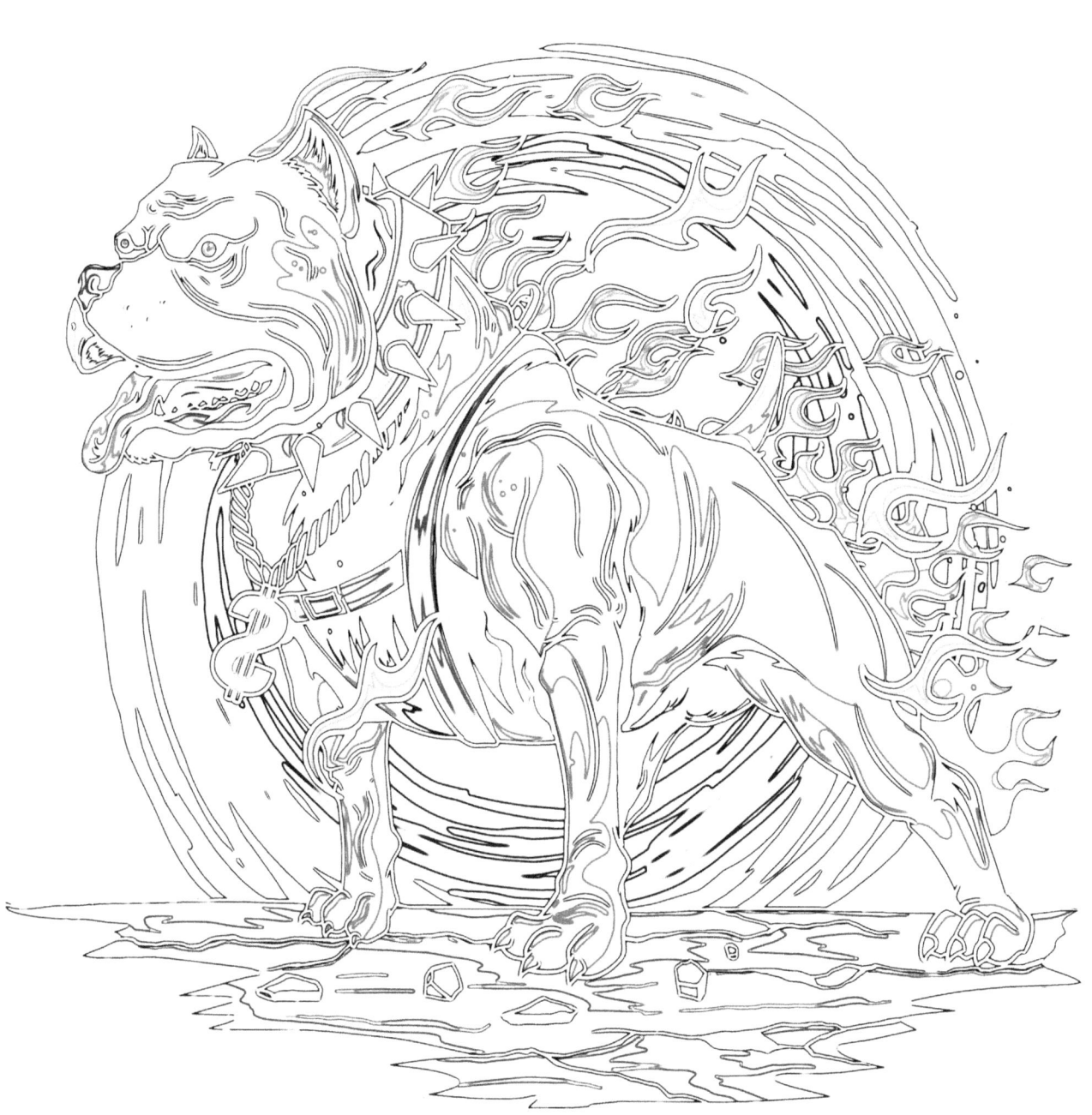

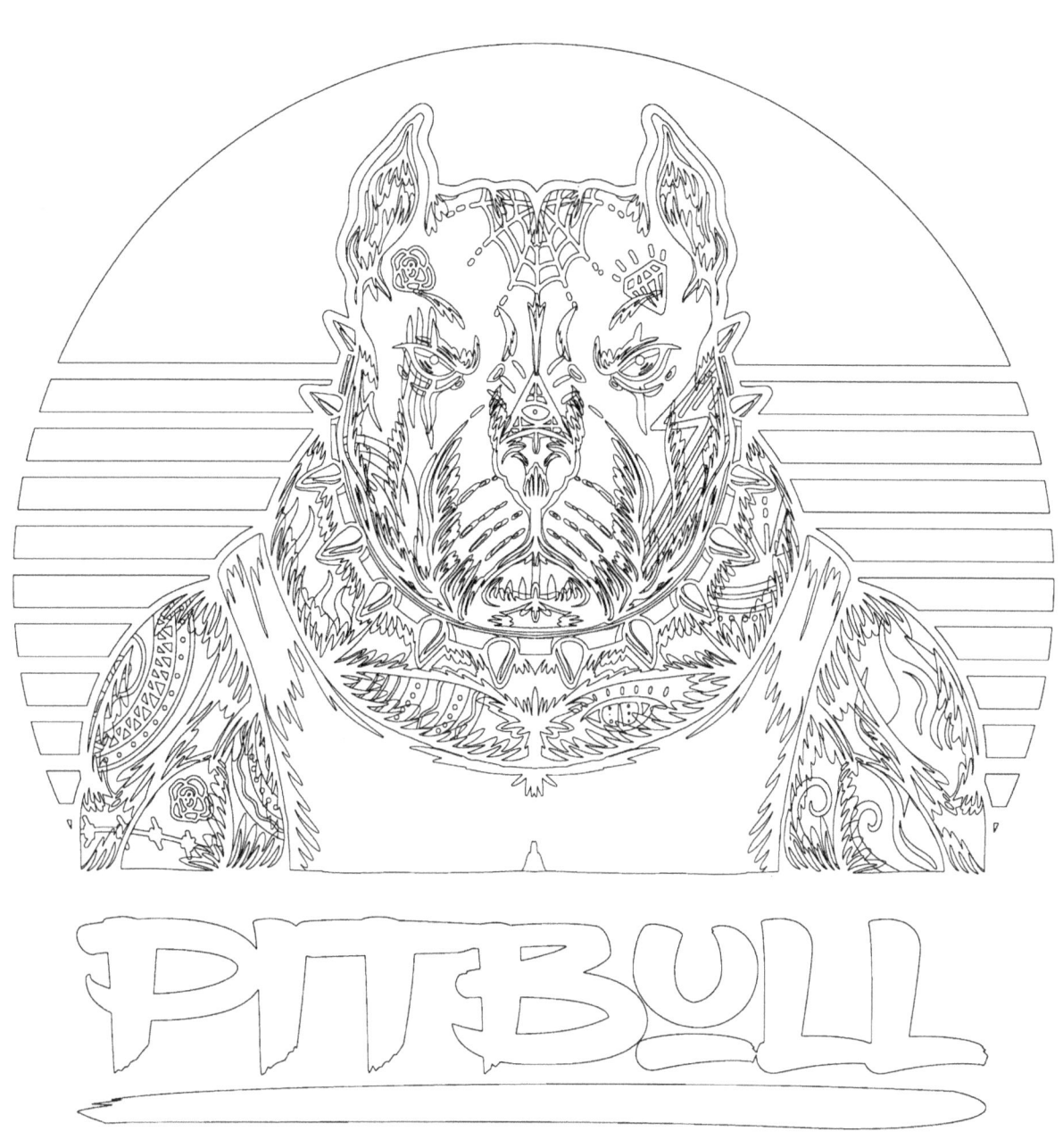

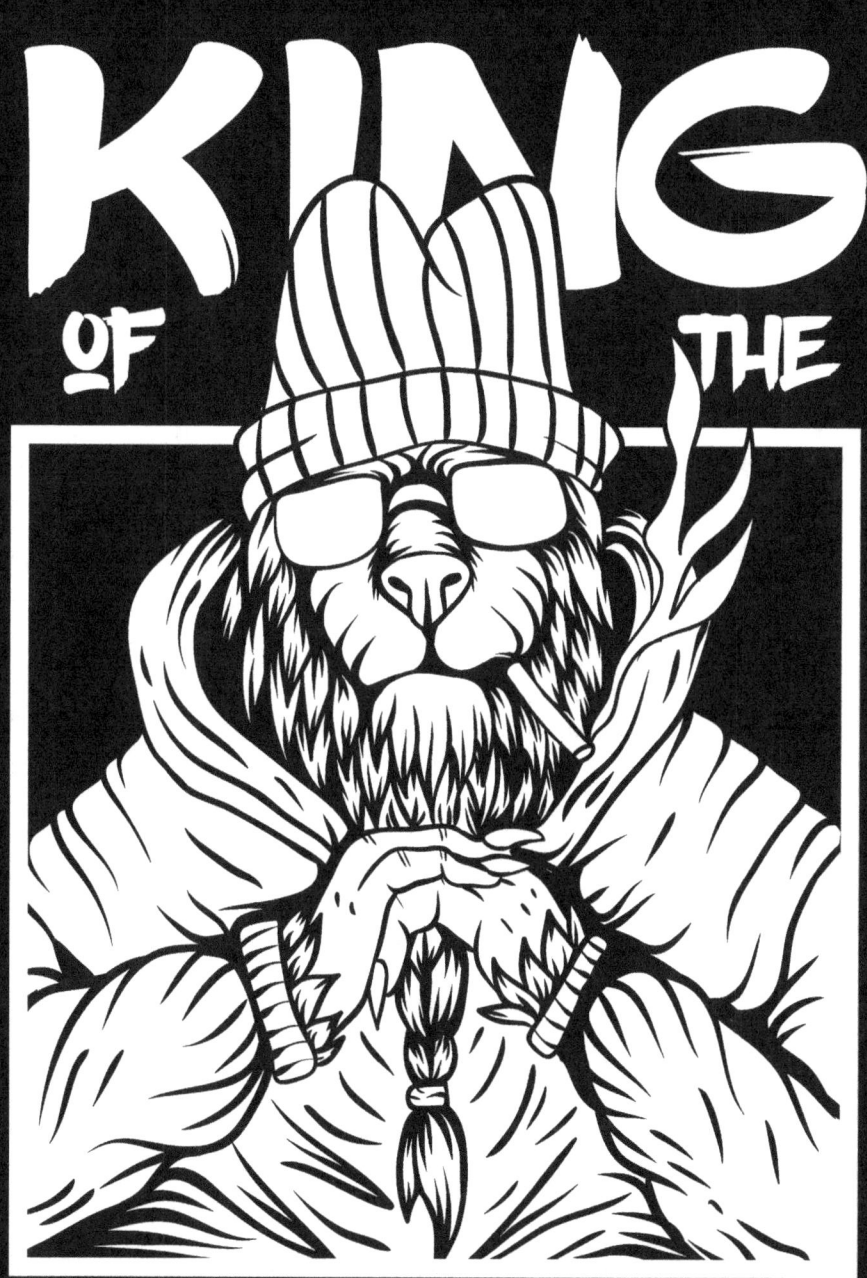

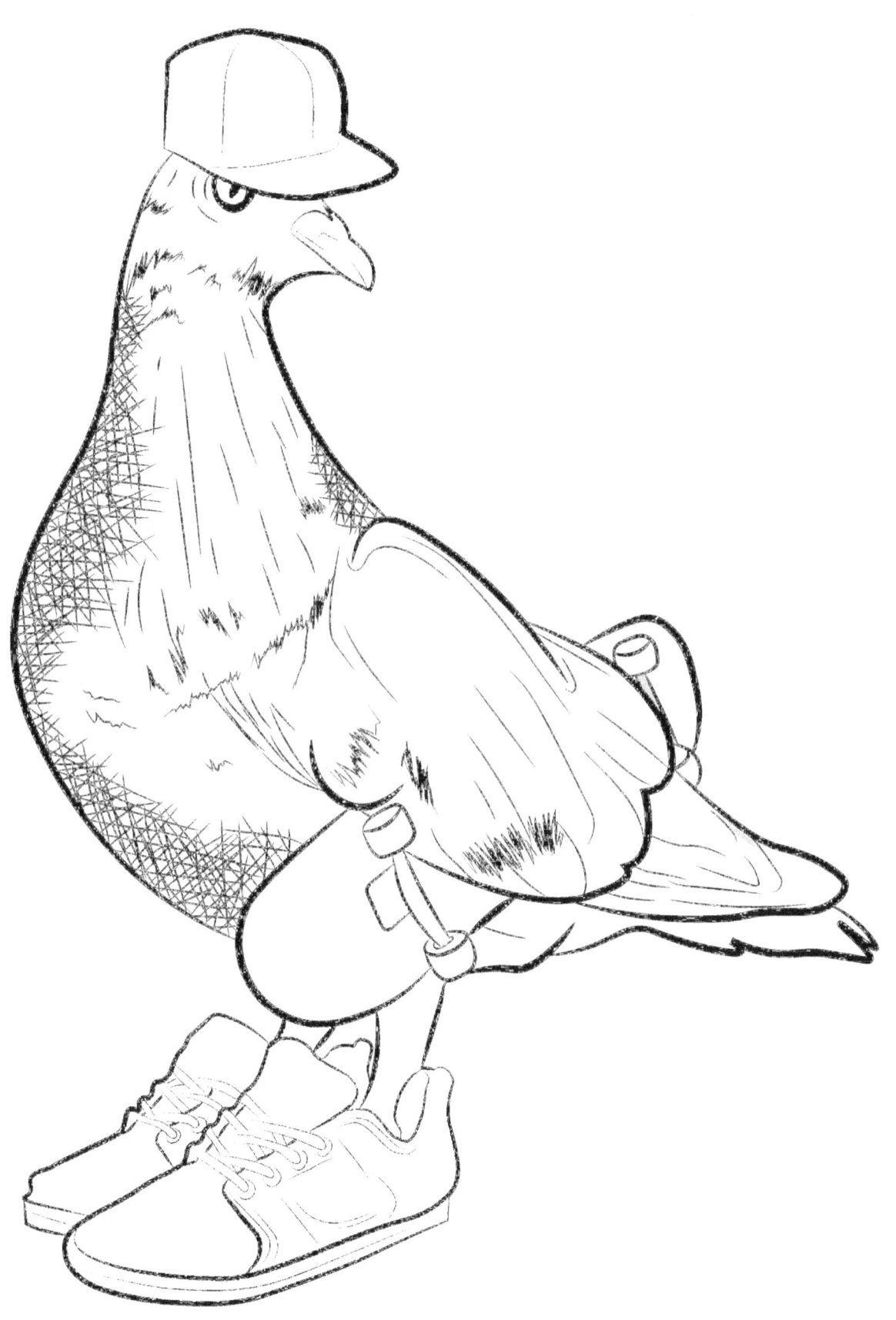

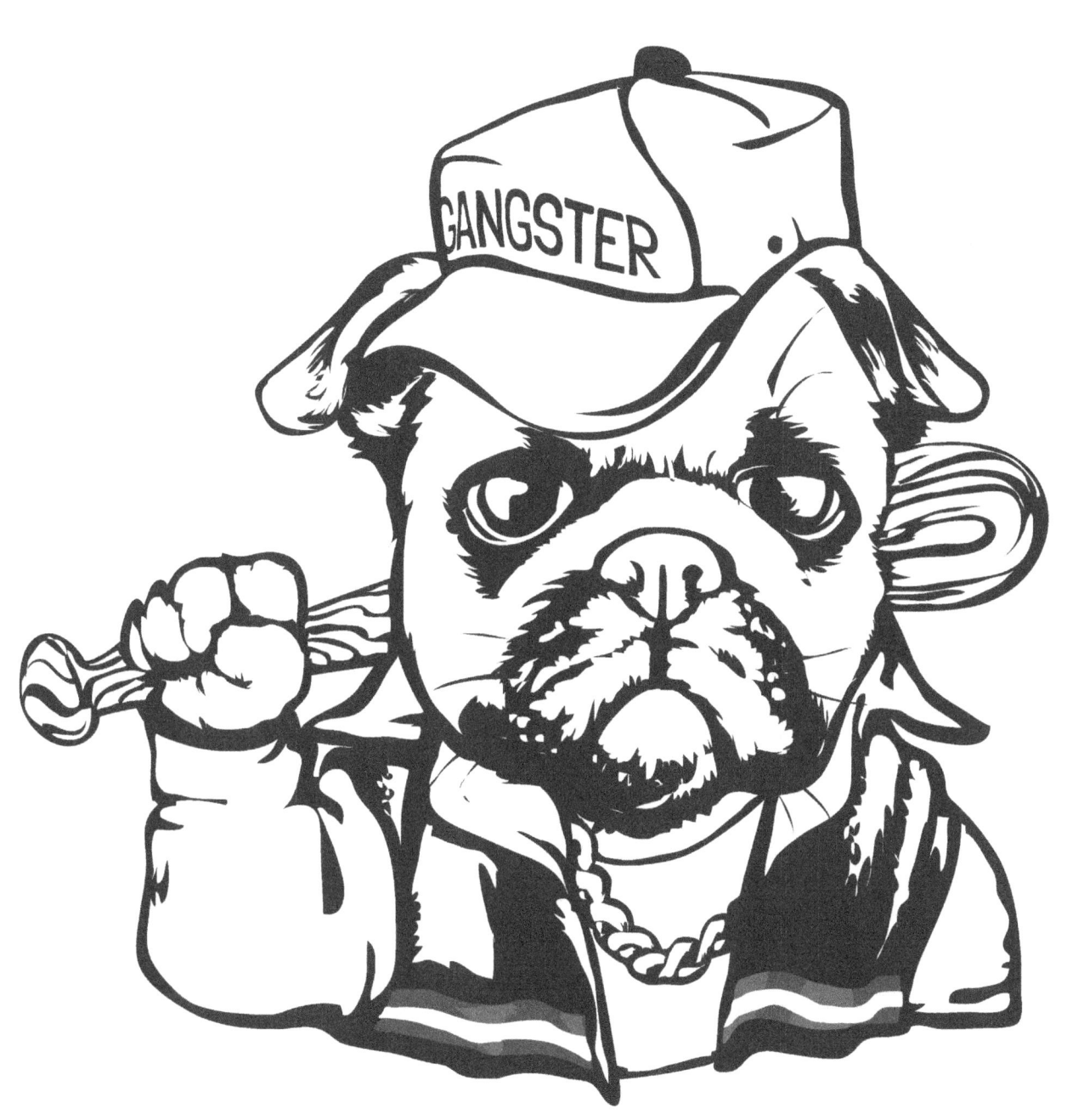

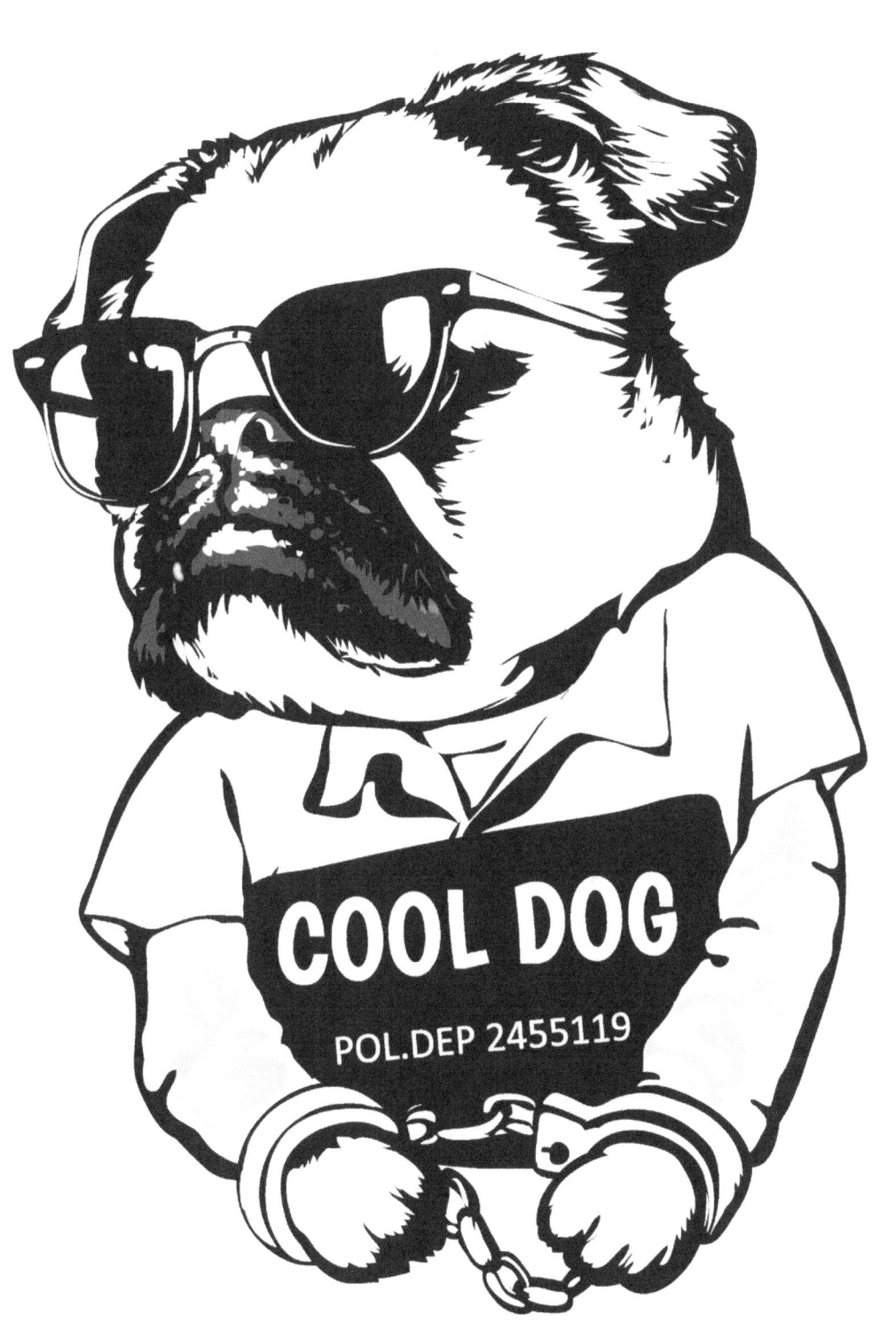

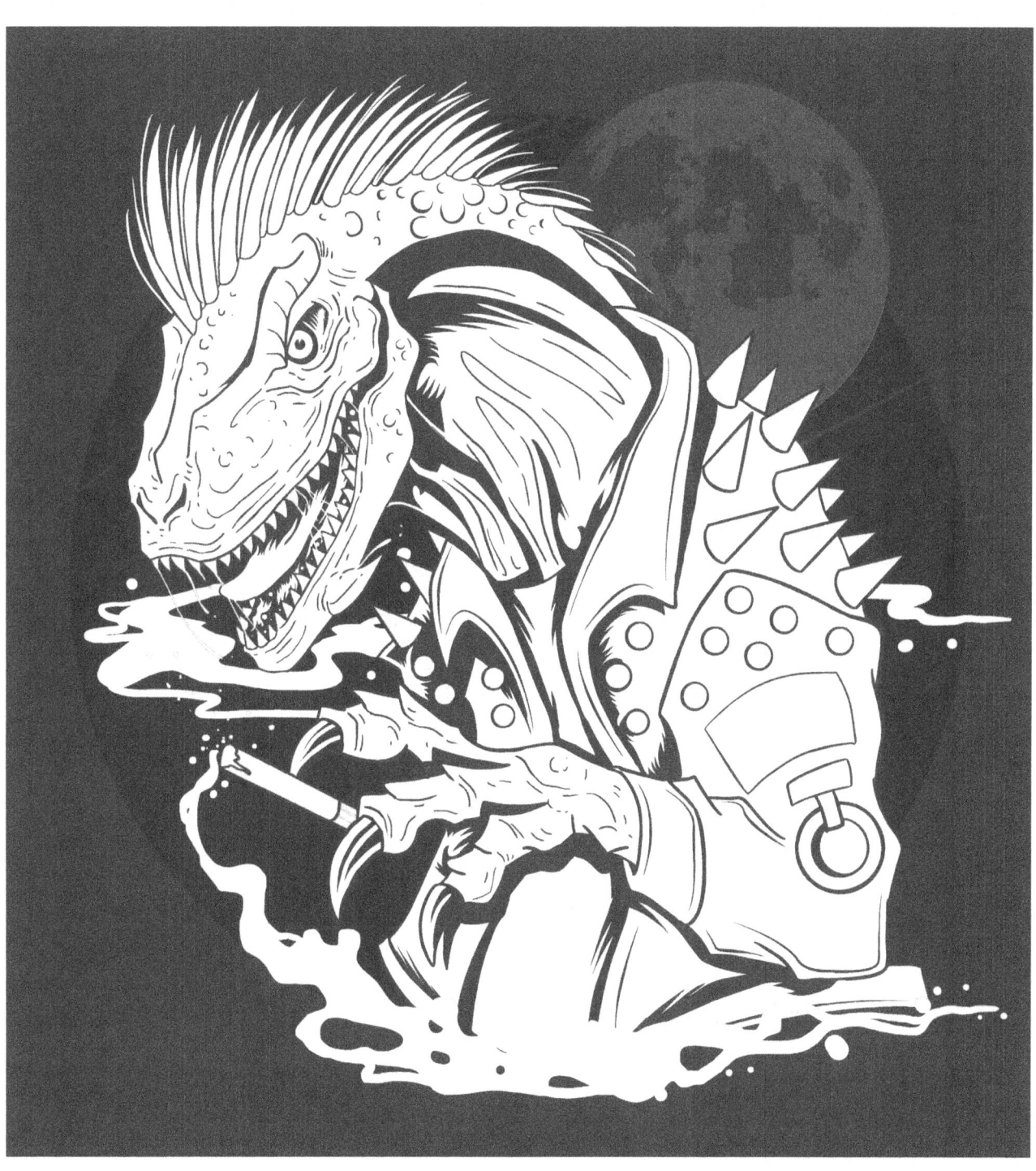

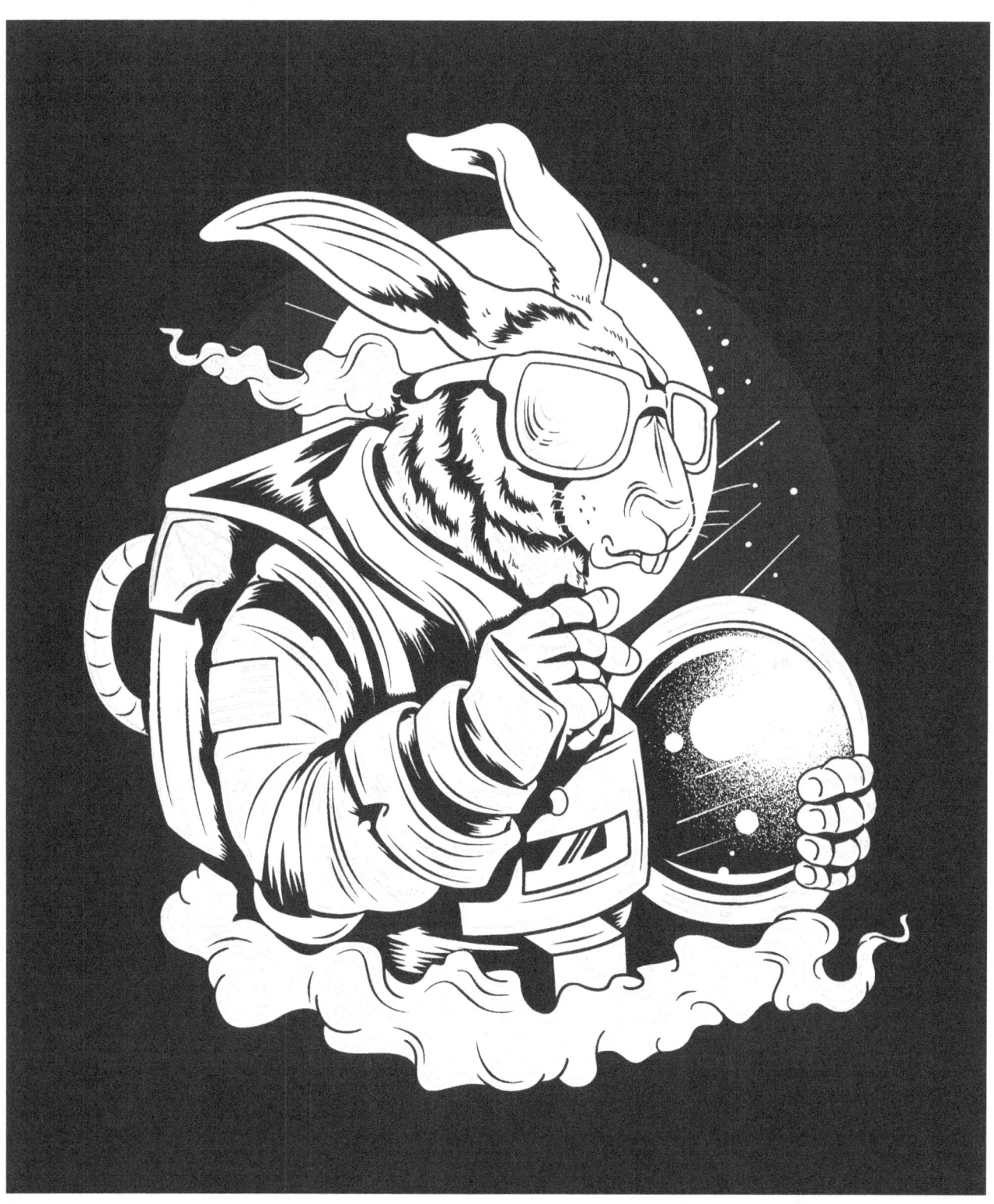

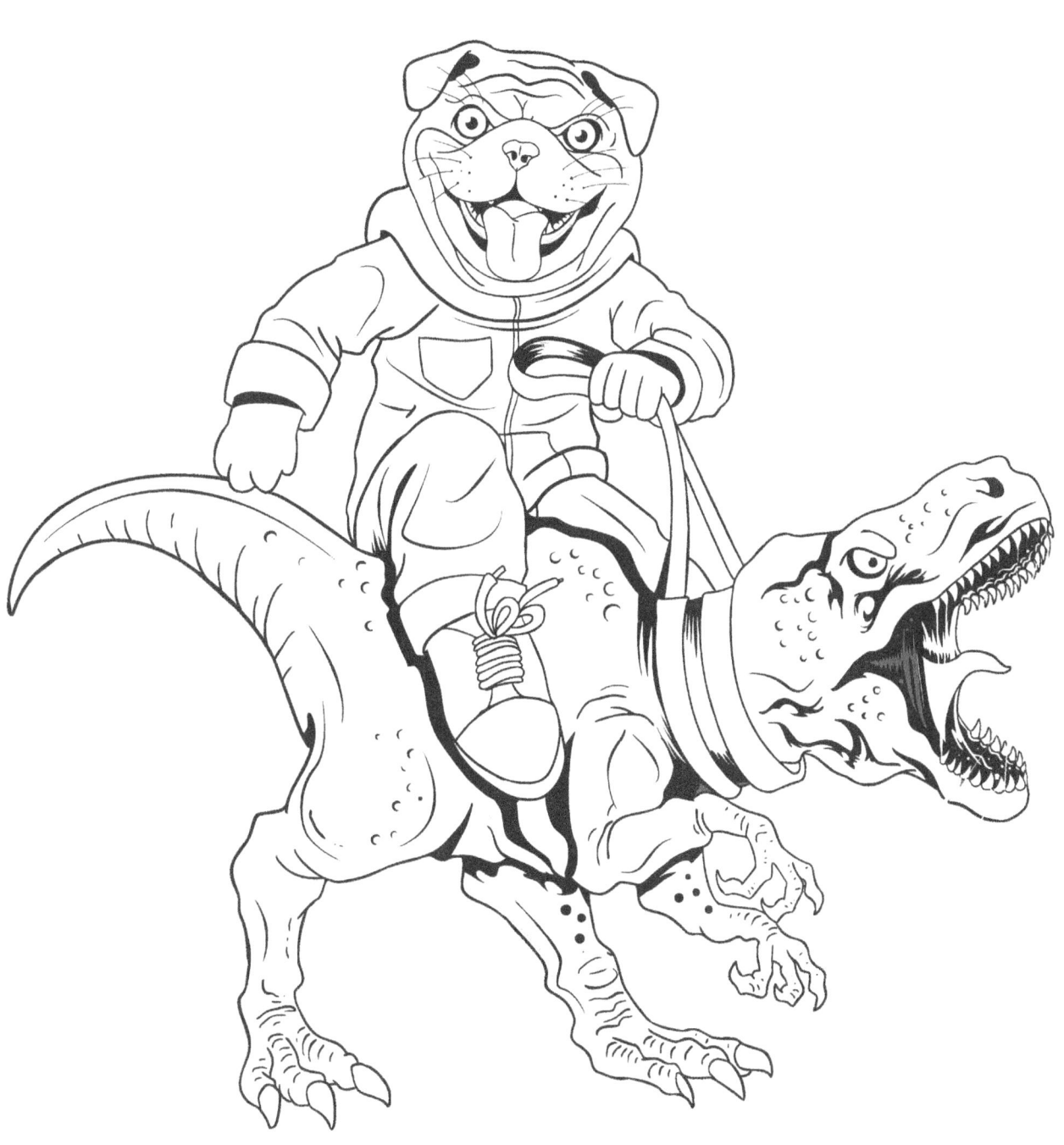

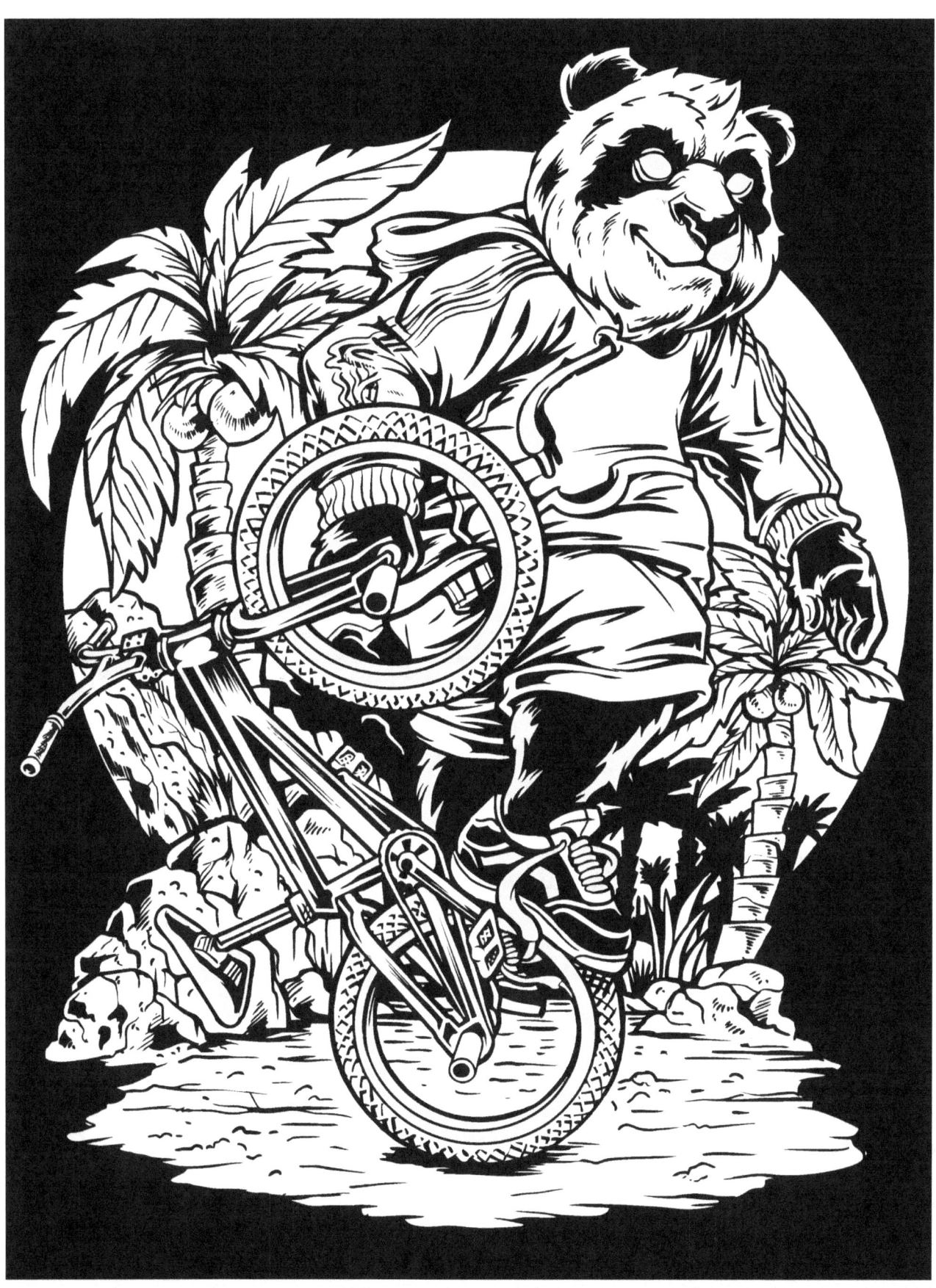

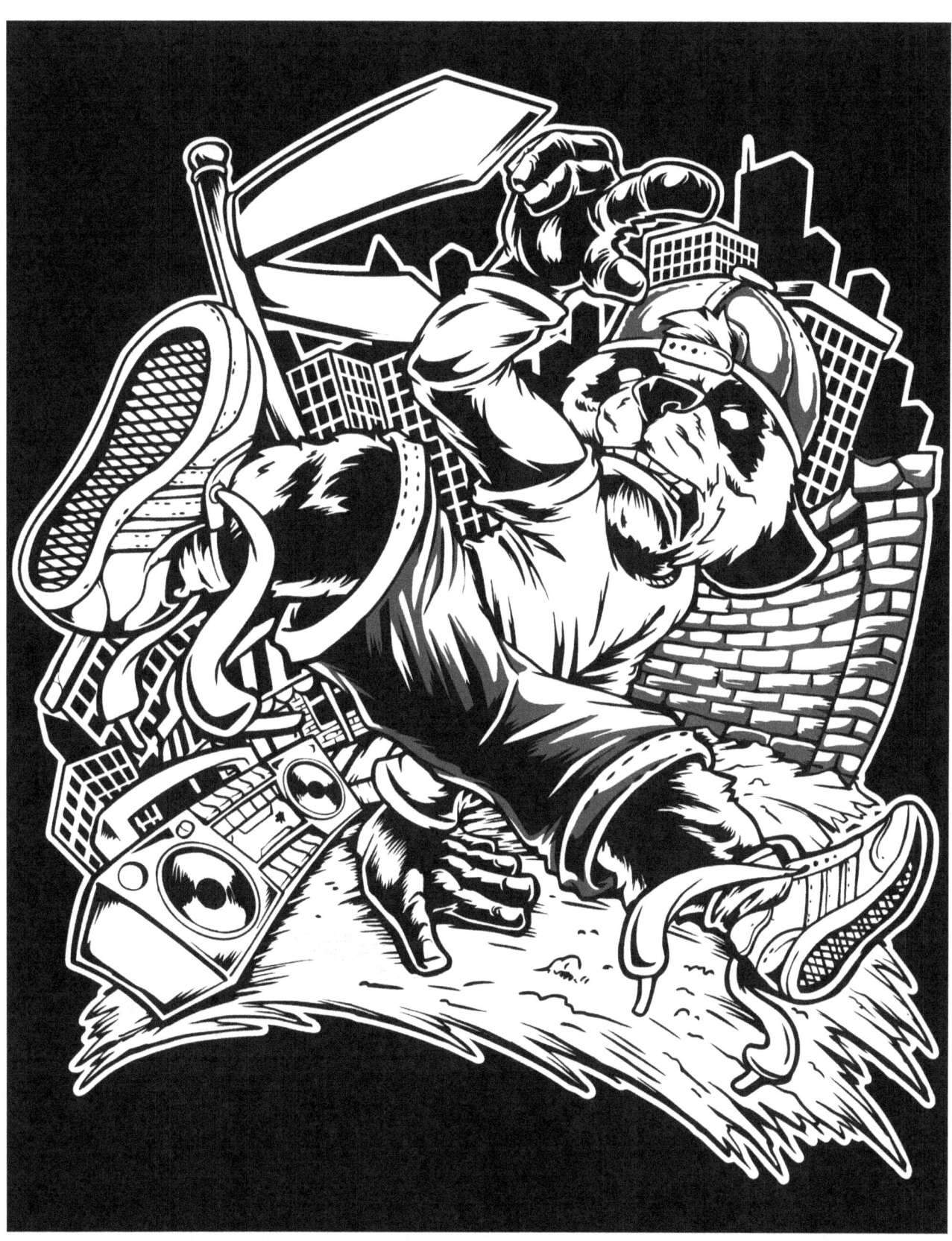

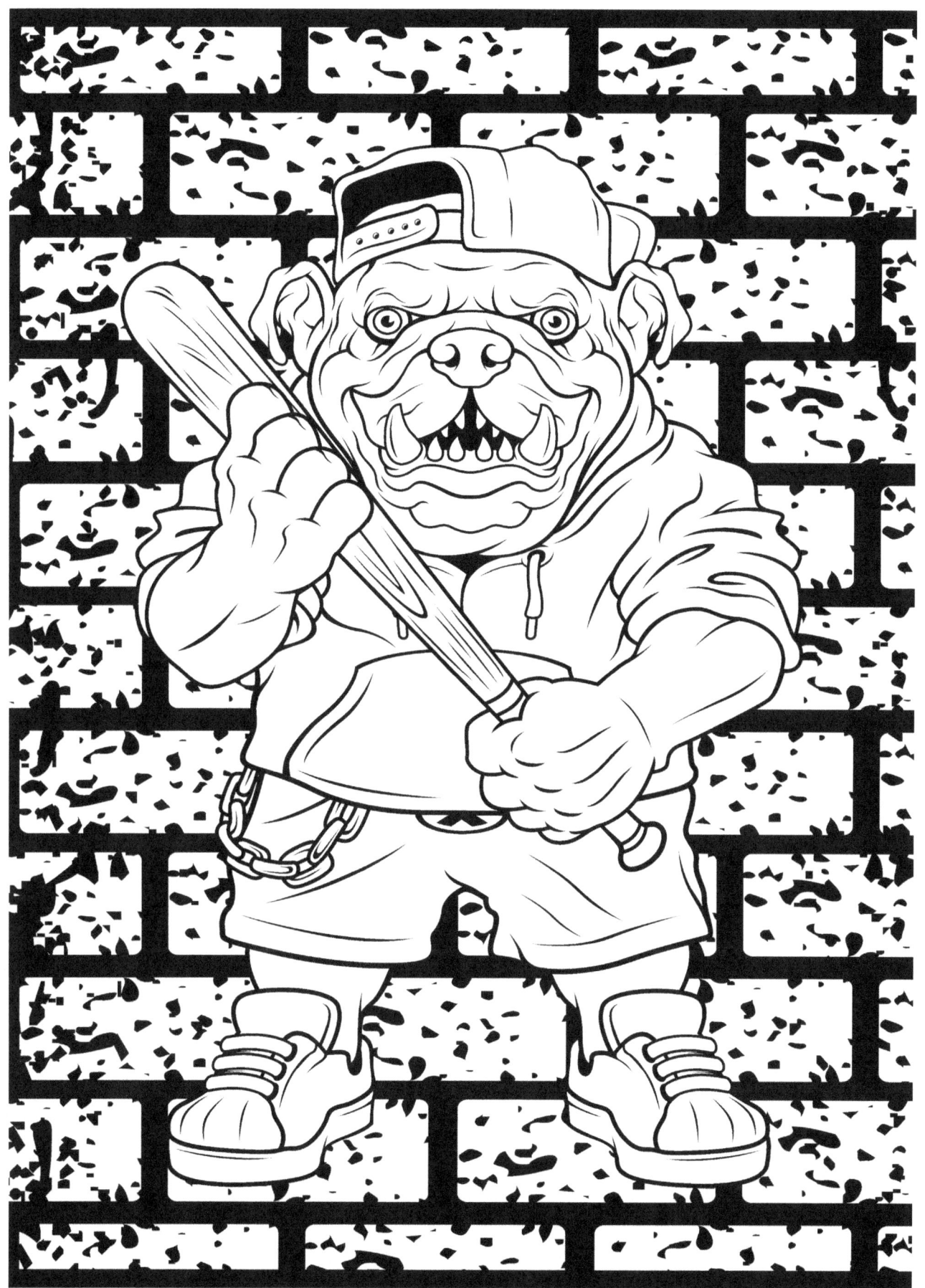

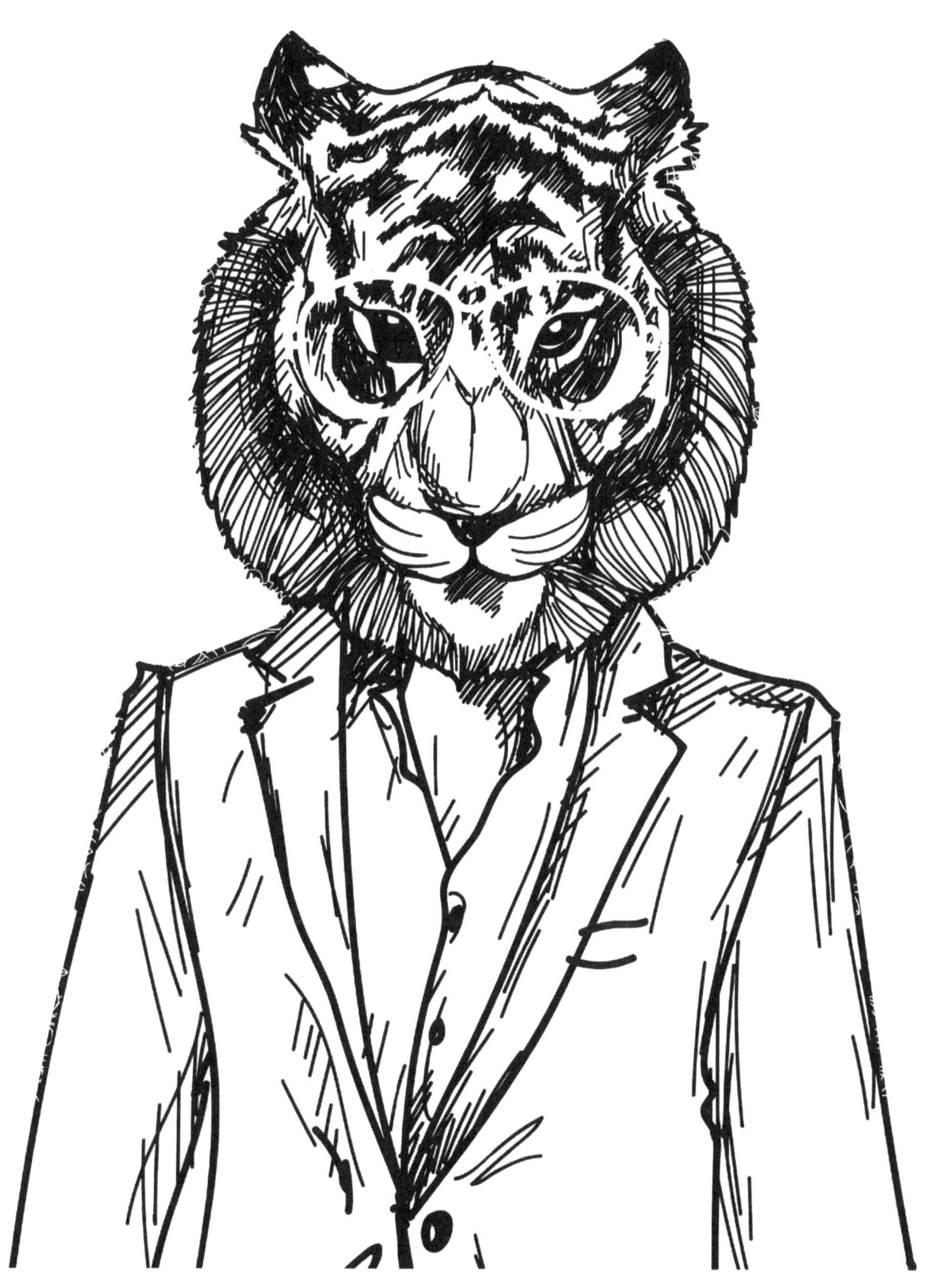

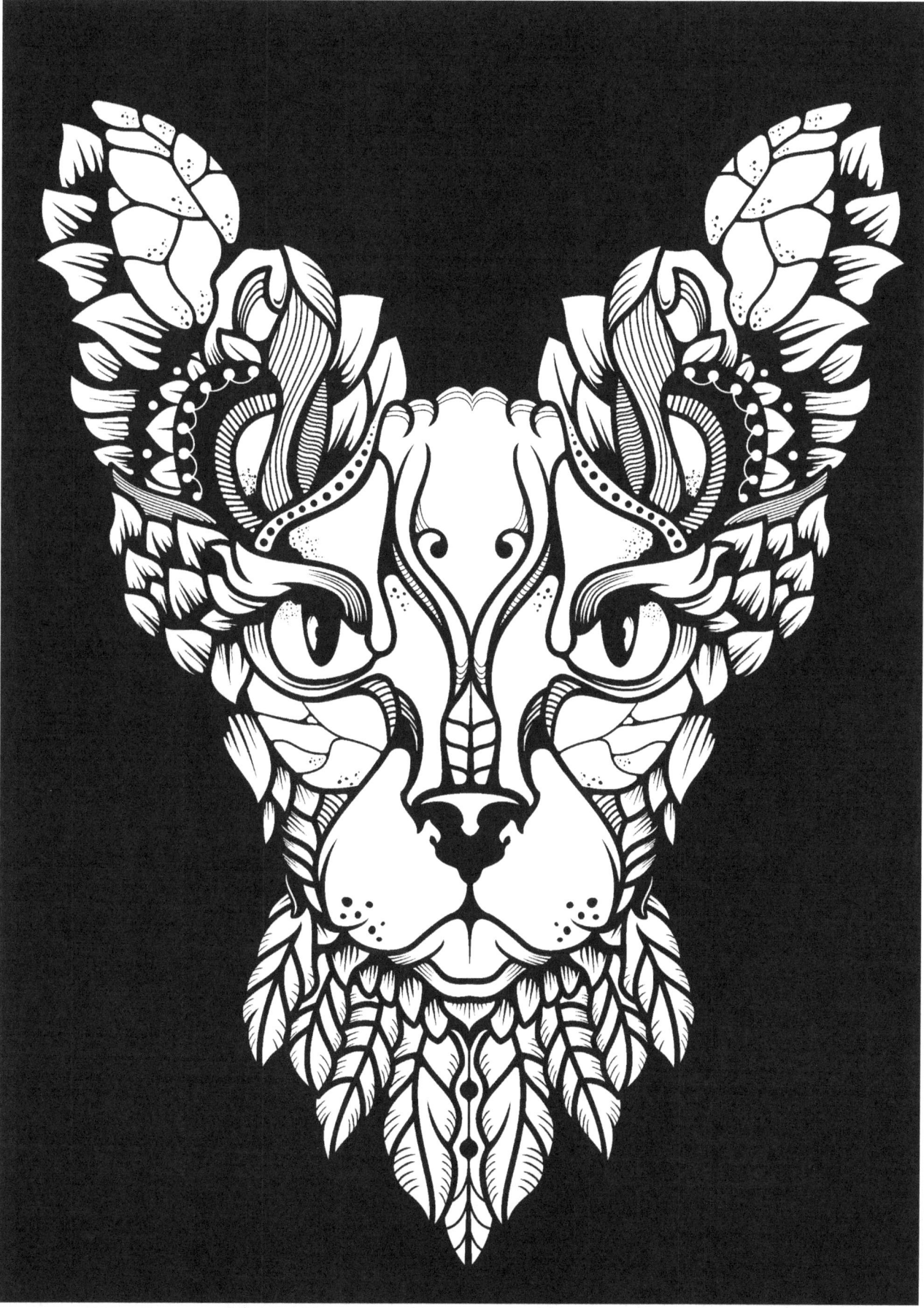

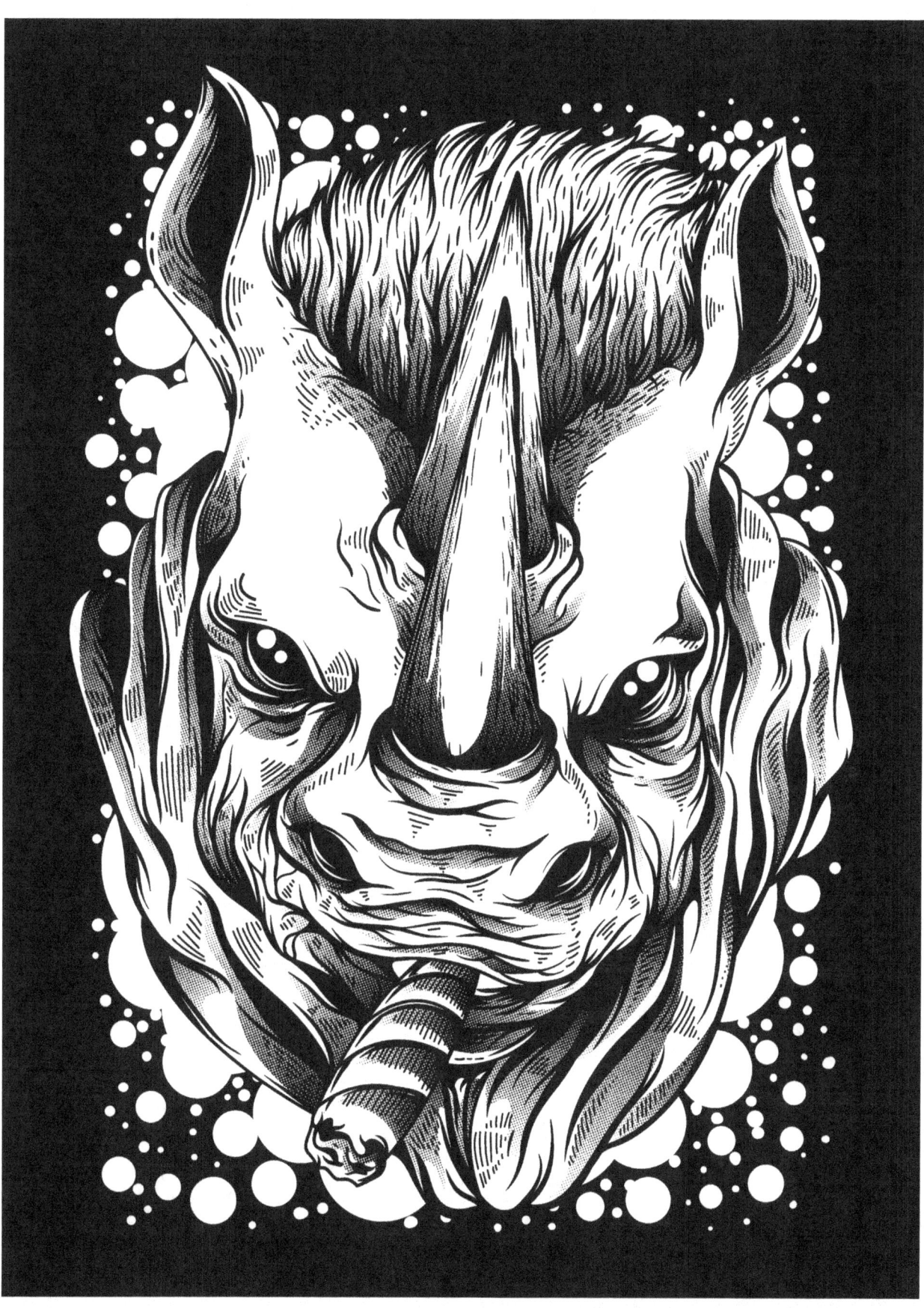

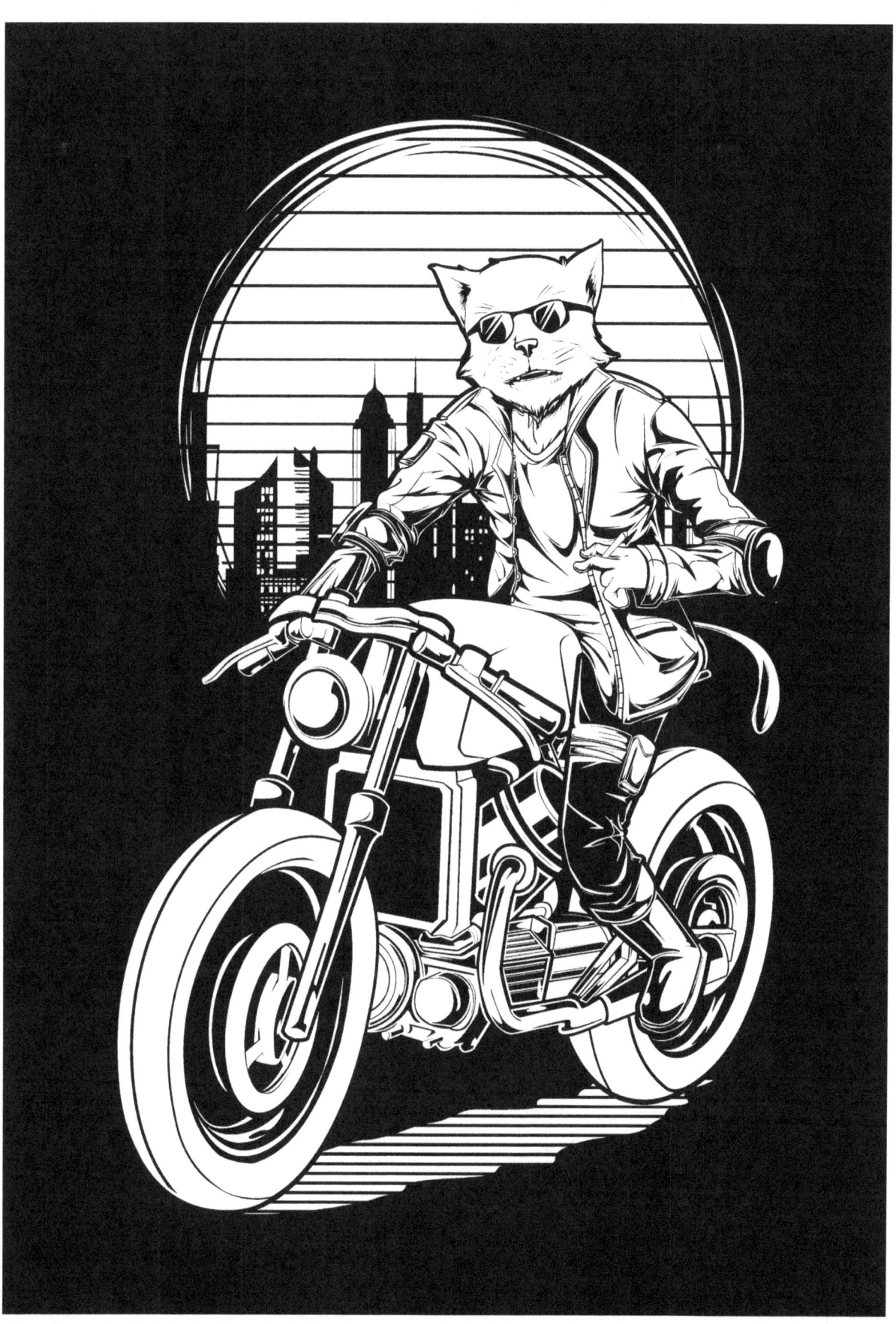

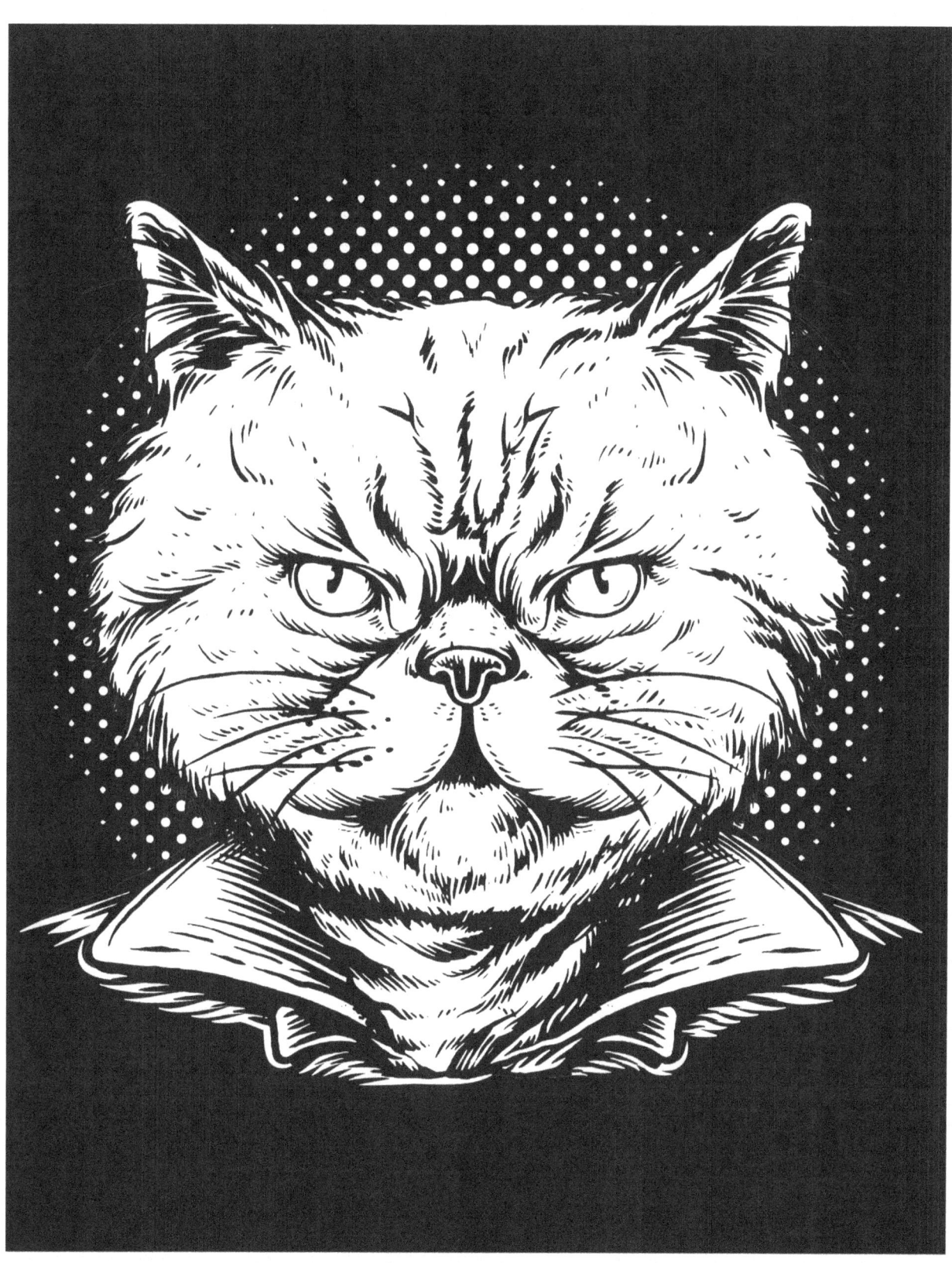

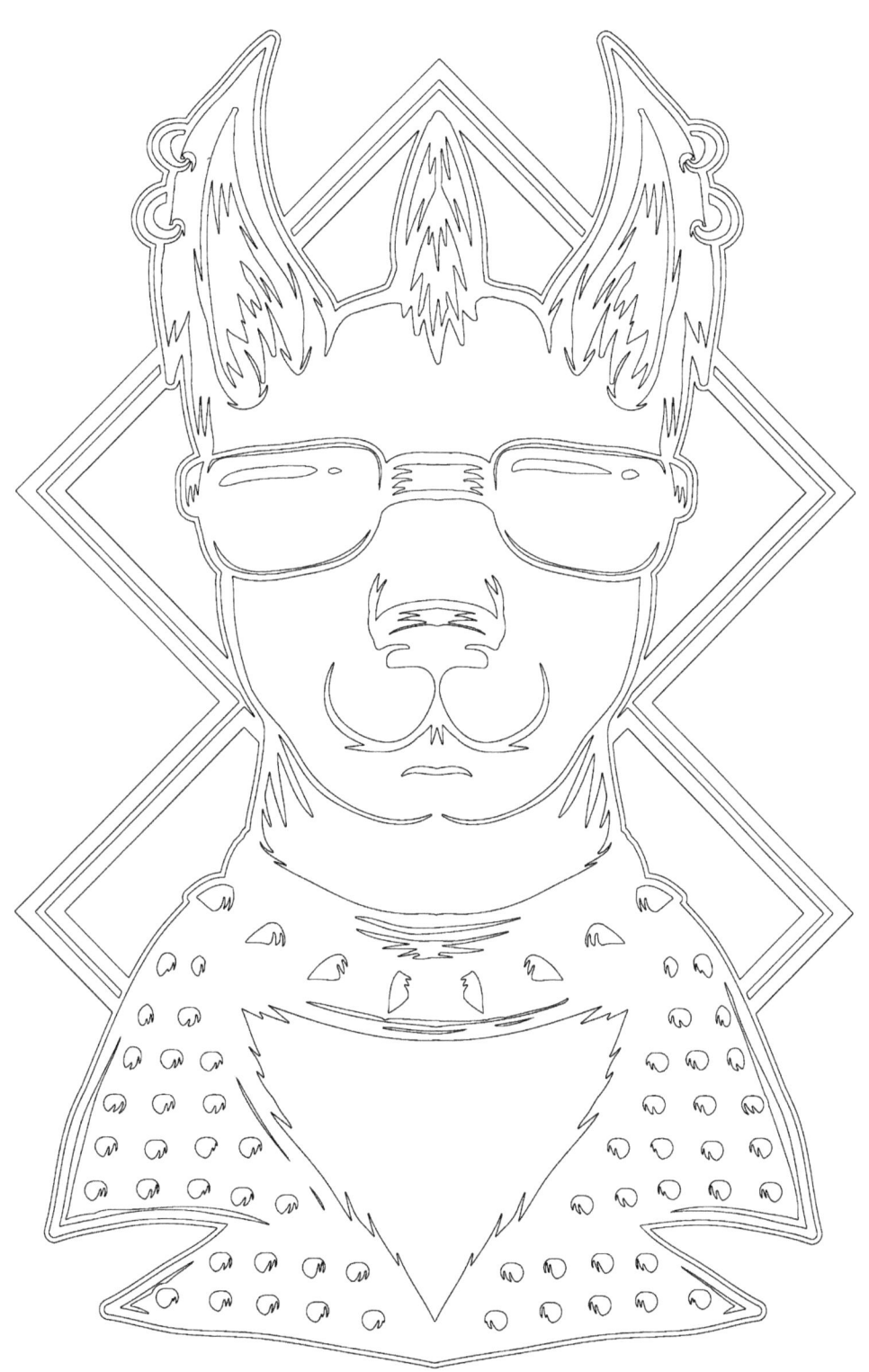

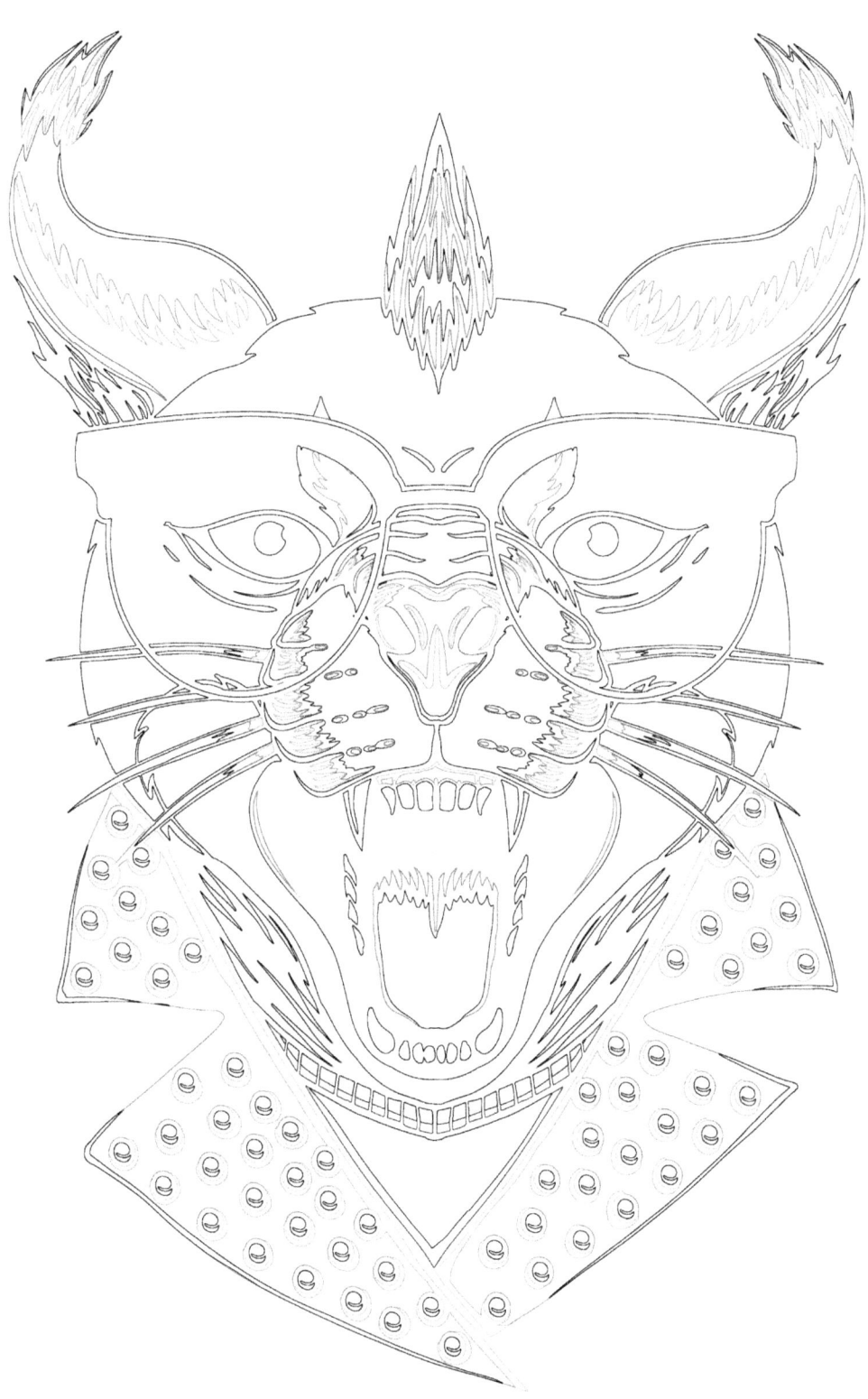

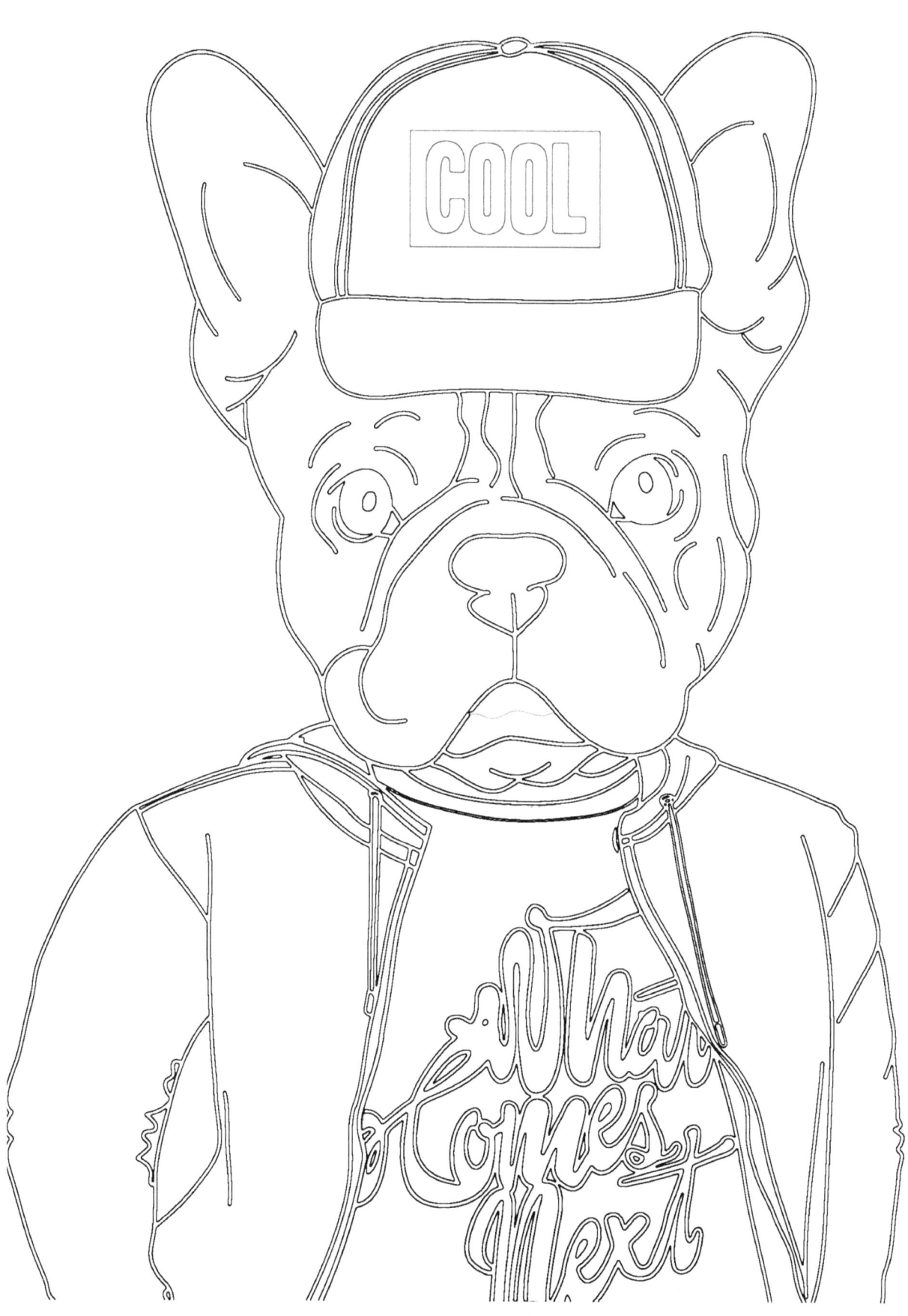

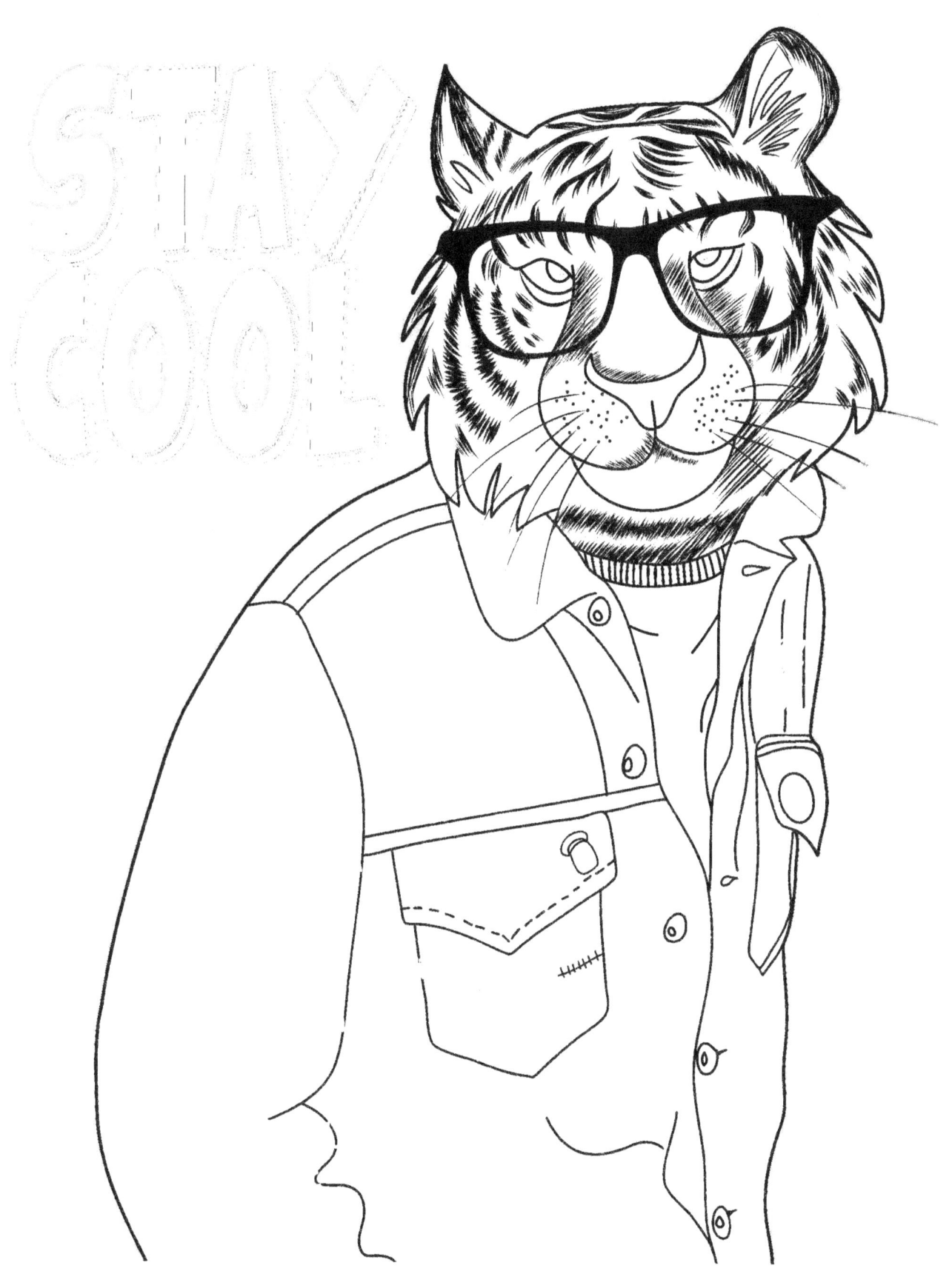

www.ingramcontent.com/pod-product-compliance
Lightning Source LLC
Chambersburg PA
CBHW081457220526

45466CB00008B/2688